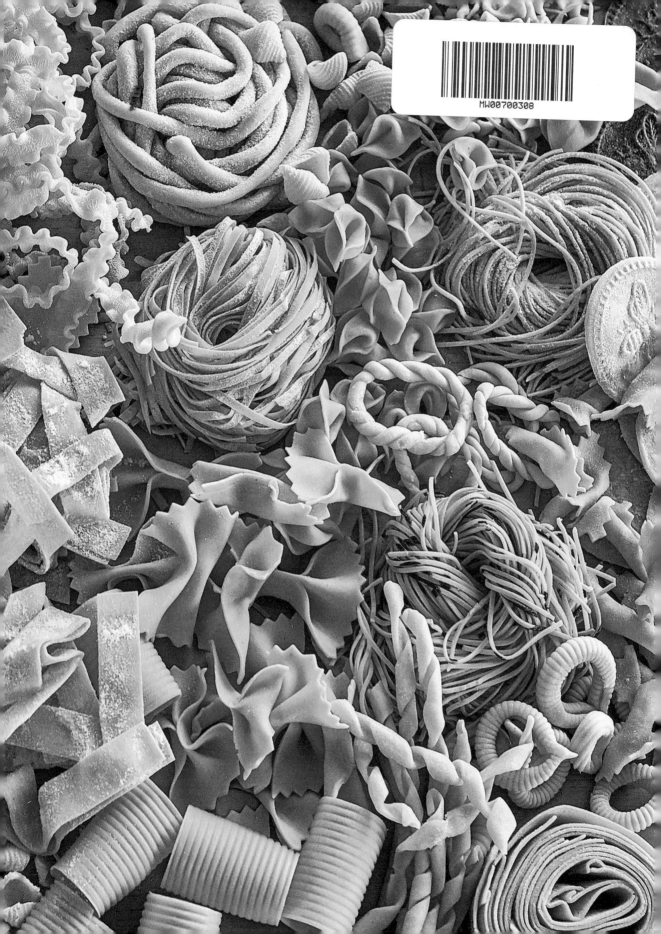

MATEO ZIELONKA

PASTA MASTERCLASS

Recipes for spectacular pasta doughs, shapes,
fillings and sauces, from The Pasta Man

DESIGN & PHOTOGRAPHY BY DAVE BROWN

Hardie Grant

QUADRILLE

MATEO ZIELONKA

PASTA MASTERCLASS

Recipes for spectacular pasta doughs, shapes,
fillings and sauces, from The Pasta Man

DESIGN & PHOTOGRAPHY BY DAVE BROWN

INTRODUCTION

I didn't grow up with the idea that one day I'd become a chef, or even an accomplished home cook. Family meals were always good, especially when there was *knedle* or *kopytka* for supper, but looking back I didn't hang around the kitchen, keen to learn or help. There was nothing to suggest that I would one day acquire the nickname 'The Pasta Man' and publish a cookbook – let alone two.

My early experiments with cooking were not auspicious. I shared a bedroom with my older brother Jakub, and sometimes I would persuade him to smuggle the sandwich-maker to bed with us. Then, when the household was settled to sleep, I would plug it in and set about making toasted cheese sandwiches. On more than one occasion my father appeared in his pyjamas, flicked on the light and caught us red-handed, given away by the scent of melted cheese. The less risky option was to save any mealtime leftovers in my Scooby-Doo lunchbox, which I would then produce from under the bed long after midnight to offer Jakub half a sausage, first brushing any stray cake crumbs from it, or to offer cake, which I hoped didn't taste too much of pork.

I think of these mismatched flavours sometimes when I'm cooking in the kitchen at 180 The Strand, musing on whether salmon might pair well with cheese, or whether pickled rhubarb would complement a duck-filled *caramelle* (it does, and it's delicious). I love Italian cooking and all things pasta-related, but I'm not Italian, so I'm less inclined to stick to some of the traditions that are so proudly adhered to in Italy. Of course, these traditions are my starting point, the basis for every cooking adventure and voyage of discovery, and I am always excited to visit Italy and learn as much as I can from people with a passion for pasta.

When my publisher suggested this book might be called *Pasta Masterclass*, I wasn't convinced I could claim to be a master of pasta-making at all. Of course, I am a pasta chef, but I feel as though I still have so much to learn; that there are so many other people out there who have wonderful skills and knowledge to share. It's an ongoing process. I think the word that really describes me best is a pasta 'enthusiast'. Enthusiasm has a habit of being infectious, and I'm always happiest when I can inspire other people to talk about pasta, to make it, cook it and eat it.

There's nothing nicer than seeing pictures online from people who've made pasta with their kids, tried their own version of a tricky shape, or when somebody who has never cooked before tells me that they've asked for a pasta machine for their birthday so they can have a go themselves. Pasta classes are fun, too; even making the simplest ribbon pasta brings smiles of pleasure as flour and eggs are transformed into beautiful golden strands. There's joy in making, whether it's food, craft or art, and to me making pasta is a combination of all three, something that is so absorbing and interesting, and which – best of all – you get to eat!

I hope you will be inspired by this book to enjoy your own pasta adventures. Put on an apron, roll up your sleeves and prepare to get a little dusty with flour. *Buon appetito!* Or as we say in Poland, *smacznego!*

EQUIPMENT

Pasta-making requires some specialist equipment, of course, but it's always wise to remember that Italian home cooks – the best pasta-makers in the world – often cook in simple kitchens with a minimum of tools. Apart from one or two things it would be hard to do without, it can be fun to improvise with what you have, and if you search your kitchen there's often a utensil that can do a job it wasn't invented for. Once you are committed to your new pasta hobby, then you can invest in the specialist accessories that you know you're going to value. I admit I'm obsessed and love trying new tools, but here's a list of some of the basics to give you an idea of where to start.

TO MAKE AND SHAPE

Pasta machine or KitchenAid attachment

If you've bought this book then I'm guessing you probably have a pasta machine, perhaps one you were given as a present that's been tucked away in a kitchen cupboard, or maybe one that's in weekly use already (in which case, *bravo, amico mio!*). Either way, you will need one to make many of the pastas in this book, unless you're a wizard with a *mattarello* (a pasta rolling pin). At home I use a Marcato Atlas 150 or 180 pasta machine, as they make a wider pasta sheet than some other brands. They are really good, solid machines, made in Italy and available worldwide. I also use a KitchenAid attachment, which is actually quicker than the machine and takes up less space (the attachment is small enough to put in the utensils drawer, helpful when space is at a premium). An important note: clean your pasta machine or the KitchenAid attachment with a damp cloth and never plunge them into the washing-up bowl or the dishwasher, which will make them seize up and stop working properly.

Mattarello (pasta rolling pin)

A longer-than-usual rolling pin designed to roll out large sheets of pasta dough. Often made from a single length of beechwood or other straight-grained wood, a *mattarello* is usually at least 80cm/31in long. The knack of rolling *sfoglia* (hand-rolled pasta dough) takes a bit of practice and I'm still learning, but like anything, the more you do it the better you get. Check online for Daniel Ewart at Nonnas Wood Shop for a whole range of beautiful tools hand-made from Canadian hardwoods like walnut and maple.

Pasta extruder

This machine mixes the pasta dough and pushes it through a bronze die inserted in the mixer attachment to create the desired shape. Extruders are mostly used commercially, but there are now several domestic versions on the market. At home, I use an Arcobaleno Vita machine, which is fantastic and makes easy work of a lot of pasta; it's compact, quick and comes with a box of dies. Pushing the dough through bronze creates a rough surface to the pasta, perfect for holding the sauce. Pasta made with semolina and water will keep for several months if it's dried properly, so it can be fun to give as a gift, packaged in a cellophane bag with your own hand-made pasta label.

Garganelli or cavarola board

This small ridged board and pin is used to make garganelli, capunti and malloreddus, and to make ridges on gnocchi. You can always improvise and use a fork instead, but look out for boards online – they are quite cheap unless you choose a specialist maker.

Ravioli cutter

An indispensable tool used to seal the edges of filled pastas such as ravioli, giving them their distinctive decorative edge. The best ravioli cutters have a brass cutting wheel and can be quite expensive, but if you make pasta regularly, they are well worth it. A note on cleaning: let the cutter dry out a little after use, then use a brush or damp cloth to clear off any residual dough. Again, don't drop it into the washing-up bowl, and definitely don't put it in the dishwasher, or the wheel will clog and seize up.

EQUIPMENT

Corzetti stamp

A two-part carved wooden tool, one half of which cuts out the pasta shape, while the other half embosses the pattern. I bought mine from master woodcarver Filippo Romagnoli at romagnolipastatools.com, who hand-carves some beautiful patterns into them.

Anolini stamp

A metal tool that comes in a range of sizes, it is used to easily stamp out *anolini*. I have a large and small version, but you can simply use a small round cookie cutters instead.

Chitarra box

I was sent my *chitarra* box as a gift and I'm a big fan. Taut wires are strung the length of a wooden box, then the dough is rolled and pushed through the wires with a rolling pin, creating fine, squared ribbons of pasta. You can only use it for making one shape, however, so don't invest unless you love *spaghetti alla chitarra*. It's also quite a chunky piece of equipment, so be sure you've got somewhere to keep it (mine lived under the bed for a while). Look online for one if you decide to make this shape.

Ferretto

'*Ferro*' means 'iron', though now these square or twisted rods are made of brass and are used to make tubular pastas such as *busiate*, *fusilli* or *maccheroni*. I use them to shape *farfalle* too.

Bicicletta

A multi-wheel dough cutter that makes short work of cutting multiple strips or squares of pasta dough and which definitely gives you that professional air. It creates a straight cut, so if you want a zig-zag edge then you need to use a *ravioli* cutter.

TO COOK PASTA AND SAUCES

Pasta pan

This refers to nothing other than a good-sized pan, one that will hold sufficient water to submerge the pasta and with plenty of room for a good rolling boil. I use a 6-litre/12½-US-pint stainless-steel pan and, although they are smart, I don't use a pasta pan with an integrated basket/strainer, as I don't have room to store one and they're not really necessary.

Pasta basket

If you do have (or want to get) a separate pasta basket, though, it's a useful way of cooking pasta – simply drop it into a pasta basket that fits inside your pan. Once the pasta is cooked, lift the basket out of the water. There's no more fishing around for escaped strands of pasta and you will always have the extra pasta cooking water you need to loosen your sauce.

Spider strainer

This is useful for scooping delicate filled pastas from the pan. A slotted spoon does the job, but if you have a wide, flat spider strainer it will lift more pasta (you don't want it hanging around in the pan longer than needed, as it risks being overcooked).

Saucepan

I like to use a wide, shallow stainless-steel casserole to cook my sauces. It has a good heavy base for frying, and the two handles help when tossing the pasta in the sauce. All you really need to bear in mind is that the cooked pasta is transferred to the sauce (not the other way round), so you need plenty of room to combine them together.

TO DRY AND STORE

Drying rack

I didn't bother using a rack until my friend Max bought me one from a charity shop – a collapsible wooden dowelling rack boxed in faded 1970s' packaging. It's useful for air-drying ribbon pastas so they don't stick together on the tray.

Drying tray

A wooden frame with a mesh base, or a perforated plastic tray, drying trays are usually designed to be stackable so you can air-dry a large quantity of pasta. Short pastas such as *malloreddus*, *lorighittas* or *corzetti* can be fully dried on trays, and well dried pasta can keep for months. If you have an extruder, it should come with its own drying tray, which you will need to dry the pasta evenly.

Airtight containers

Fresh egg short and ribbon pastas will keep for three to four days if stored properly. Dust the pasta with semolina flour and place in an airtight container, which should then be kept in the fridge. Ideally, filled pastas should be eaten the day they are made or at least within a day of making. *Ravioli* made a day ahead should be dusted with semolina and stored on a tray in the fridge. Eggless semolina pasta, when it's dried correctly, will keep for months in an airtight container in your store cupboard.

GENERAL KITCHEN UTENSILS

A **food processor** is a good kitchen assistant. Whether it's making pasta dough or sauces, pesto or *pangrattato*, it speeds up every job. I still hate washing them up afterwards, though.

A **dough scraper** is pretty much indispensable. I use a hard plastic one to scoop dough from the work surface, while a metal one has a sharper cutting edge for when I want to cut doughs with precision.

I keep a metal **ruler** handy to measure out squares and ribbons of pasta and use a **pastry or cookie cutter** to cut circles of dough for shapes such as *anolini* or *campanelle*.

Use a **piping bag** with a narrow nozzle to fill delicate pastas. Soft fillings are slightly compressed when forced through a nozzle, which is handy when you're working with smaller shapes.

A **pastry brush** dipped in water helps seal the edges of filled pasta, while a **spray bottle** is useful if your pasta dough is drying out in a warm kitchen; a spritz of water can make it pliable again.

Invest in a sharp **Parmesan grater**. I couldn't do without a microplane – they have such a fine cutting edge, and are stylish enough to take to the table along with a chunk of Parmesan so your guests can help themselves.

THE PASTA
STORE CUPBOARD

These are the basic ingredients in my store cupboard, so I am always ready to make pasta at home at a moment's notice.

ITALIAN 00 FLOUR

This is finely milled flour that has been ground twice, and is perfect for making a really smooth, pliable egg dough. Mercato Italiano sell my favourite 00 flour, made by Molino Pasini (a name well worth looking out for), whose mill is in Modena, northern Italy.

FINE SEMOLINA

Known as *semolina rimacinata* or *semola*, this is twice-milled semolina that makes a really smooth, fine dough. I use it to make eggless vegan semolina dough, and for extruded pastas, too.

COARSE SEMOLINA

I use this to dust pasta dough that needs drying out a little, as the semolina absorbs moisture from the dough. It's also useful for dusting on finished shapes, as it helps to prevent them from sticking. Be generous with it, then simply sift the semolina after you've finished shaping your pasta and store it in an airtight container – it can be reused three times before it being discarded.

EGGS

I use medium eggs in all my recipes. Medium eggs should weigh around 50–55g/2oz, so if your eggs weigh less than this then adjust the quantity of flour you use, otherwise you may find your dough is on the dry side. The ratio of flour to egg should be 2 to 1 (100g/3½oz flour to 50g/2oz egg). I'm lucky to have free-range, rich-yolk eggs from St Ewe's in Cornwall, which you may be able to track down (or look for eggs labelled rich-yolk on the box). The yolks make a beautiful golden dough, a colour even more pronounced if you make rich egg dough (page 33), which has extra yolks in it. The leftover egg whites can be saved for meringue, mousse, or friands, or can simply be added to scrambled egg.

Other useful notes:

Other kitchen staples for me include **olive oil** (first cold-pressed olive oil adds a wonderful flavour to sauces; look out for the Nicolas Alziari brand in their beautiful Provençal cans). **Lemons**, a jar of **anchovies** in oil, **capers**, bulbs of **garlic**, **chilli** flakes – any of these in various combinations will make a simple pasta sauce for a quick midweek supper. I also have several **cans of tomatoes** in the cupboard for the days when it's comforting to make a slow-cooked tomato sauce (I love the sound of the sauce gently popping on the hob while I shape pasta). If the tomatoes taste a little acidic, just add a dash of good balsamic vinegar. A pot of **fresh basil** is always a cheering addition to the kitchen windowsill in summer, though the plant is usually reduced to stalks quite quickly in our house.

SALT & PEPPER

In these recipes I only give seasoning quantities where a particular amount is required. Salts vary, and it's up to you to add and check the seasoning according to your own taste. For the pasta cooking water, use everyday table salt. It's more intense – saltier – and a lot cheaper than the more the more expensive sea salt flakes, which I use to finish a dish. Pepper is always freshly ground black pepper.

PARMESAN

Who doesn't love a blizzard of Parmesan on a plate of pasta? Look for the Parmigiano-Reggiano stamp on the rind, and try to find Parmesan that has been matured for a minimum of 24 months, which has such a beautiful depth of flavour and classic grainy texture. Keep any leftover rinds in the freezer, as they are perfect for making broth (page 246) or to add flavour to soups and bean stews. Parmesan is also available as a vegetarian cheese made without animal rennet, which you can usually find stocked in good supermarkets or specialist cheese shops.

PECORINO

This sheep's-milk cheese has a subtler, softer flavour than Parmesan. It's a younger cheese which I like just as much as, if not more than, Parmesan. It's slightly creamier and very good grated over a finished pasta dish.

NUTRITIONAL YEAST FLAKES

A great vegan alternative to Parmesan, seriously addictive, and especially good on broths or scattered over a dressed green salad. If you want to change things up a little, add a handful of toasted pine nuts to the flakes.

HOW TO COOK PASTA

Hands up if you read my first book *The Pasta Man*. Yes? In which case, you may want to skip this familiar advice about how to cook pasta; just get your apron on and start cooking.

If you haven't read it, then it's worth going over the basic rules to make sure you cook your pasta just right.

THE COOKING WATER

Use a large pan to cook your fresh pasta as the water should be able to circulate around the pasta, otherwise it will not cook evenly and can clump together. I use about 4 litres/8½ US pints of water for four portions of pasta – so 1 litre/2 US pints for every 100g/3½oz of pasta.

Season the water heavily. Pasta is made from just egg, flour or semolina, and water, so any seasoning is absorbed from the cooking water and from the sauce it's served with.

I use table salt to season the cooking water once it's boiling (if you add the salt to cold water it simply takes longer to boil). I don't recommend a particular quantity of salt – they vary in flavour and intensity – but the water should taste as salty as sea water.

COOKING FRESH SHORT AND RIBBON PASTA

The most important advice I can give you is to make sure your sauce is cooked and ready to go when you start boiling the pasta; this avoids you overcooking the pasta while you wait for the sauce to heat.

Always drop the pasta into the water when the water is boiling steadily. Don't be impatient and add it too soon or the pasta won't cook perfectly.

If you're not using a pasta basket, transfer the cooked pasta from the pan to the sauce using kitchen tongs, or simply strain it through a sieve (if you do this, always make sure you reserve a jugful of the precious cooking water first). Using kitchen tongs means that some of the cooking water is carried into the sauce, which is exactly what

you want; the lovely starchy water helps the sauce cling to each strand of pasta.

Add half a ladleful of pasta cooking water at a time to a sauce, so you don't make it too sloppy. Sauces can absorb more liquid than you might think, however, so don't be too shy with the water. A walnut sauce is particularly thirsty, for example, whereas a tomato sauce may already be quite loose. You'll soon learn what you like.

I prefer to toss the pasta and sauce together rather than stirring it, which is why I generally cook sauces in a wide shallow pan with two handles. If you're not sure about tossing hot pasta and you don't want your supper landing at your feet (never a good plan), then try the tossing action using a saucepan of dry rice (it's much easier to sweep rice from the floor if you get it everywhere!). Alternatively, use tongs or a spatula to simply turn the pasta until it's well coated in the sauce.

As always, taste the finished dish to see if you like the texture and the seasoning, and adjust it with more salt or more cooking water if needed before serving.

COOKING FILLED PASTA

When you've spent an hour or two shaping *ravioli* or *caramelle*, the last thing you want to do is watch them split open in a crowded saucepan. You may find it easier to cook the pasta in two batches, one after the other, transferring each batch to the sauce once cooked. It's probably best to use one large pan if you can, but just try to work as quickly and carefully as possible, dropping the pasta into the water in small handfuls so that they cook evenly.

Once the pasta is cooked, lift it out of the water using a slotted spoon, reserving the pasta cooking water until you've combined the pasta with the sauce. The sauce may need loosening, but add the water a little at a time, moving the pasta gently around the pan so that the parcels don't split.

COOKING DRIED PASTA

As with fresh pasta, add dried pasta to steadily boiling salted water. Follow the cooking time specified on the packet, but check it a minute or two before the time stated. I like the pasta a little *al dente* and it will finish cooking in the accompanying sauce anyway.

Don't leave the pasta sitting in the cooking water. Drain it straightaway by tipping it into a colander or sieve, always making sure you keep a jugful of the pasta cooking water before it's all tipped down the sink.

FREEZING PASTA

Pasta tends to dry out a bit in the freezer, so I avoid freezing it unless absolutely necessary.

To freeze pasta dough, wrap it tightly in clingfilm (plastic wrap) – I know it's not reusable, but it keeps the pasta fresher than any other method. To defrost, take the dough out of the freezer the evening before you want to use it and leave it to slowly defrost in the fridge. The dough will have a slightly different consistency to fresh when you come to roll it, but don't worry; if it crumbles as you first put it through the machine, simply bring it together with your hands and try rolling it again.

I don't freeze ribbon pastas at all, as they can be brittle and then break when they are defrosted (which doesn't look nice on the plate). Filled pastas are best if they are blanched before freezing, as they will keep longer; it's a chore but it does work. Blanch in boiling seasoned water for 10 seconds, then plunge into iced water straightaway. Drain, and when cold and dried a little, place on a tray lined with baking parchment. Freeze on the tray, then transfer them to a container. To cook, simply drop the frozen pasta into boiling salted water and allow an extra minute's cooking time.

HOW TO FINISH YOUR PASTA DISH

Take the time to warm your plates or pasta bowls before serving. Pasta can cool quite rapidly and a warmed dish will always help.

Parmesan is usually the perfect way to finish your pasta, but *pangrattato* (page 248) and nutritional yeast flakes are both great alternatives. These options are not only for vegans – I often use them.

A real indulgence is to add half a creamy *burrata* to a portion of pasta. This delicate Italian cows' milk cheese, made from mozzarella and cream, is perfect topped with a little sea salt, fresh black pepper and a drizzle of olive oil.

You can also finish your pasta dish with vibrant green oil (page 249), which is particularly pretty drizzled over a *burrata*.

There is nothing nicer than finishing your meal with a piece of bread. In Italy, this is called *fare la scarpetta* – using a piece of soft bread to mop up your plate, especially after a creamy pasta sauce. It's a custom that I'm really fond of and one we grew up with at home.

I like to balance a meal of pasta with a bowl of greens. I think it's nice to keep it simple, just some blanched broccoli or a fresh green salad. And of course, a beer or a glass of wine is never a bad idea!

THE
PASTA
DOUGHS

CLASSIC EGG DOUGH

**Makes 400g/14oz,
enough to serve 4**

210g/7½oz Italian 00 flour

90g/3¼oz fine semolina

3 eggs

You can make classic pasta dough using just Italian 00 flour and eggs, but I find that adding a little fine semolina creates a more stable dough. It's not as soft as a full-flour version but is easier to roll and shape, and when cooked it has a little more bite. If you're already happy making dough using only 00 flour, then you may want to stick to it, but if you're just starting out or you'd like to try a new version, this one is now my go-to recipe.

If, when you are kneading the dough, it feels quite stiff and difficult to work, don't give up. It will become more elastic the more you work it. Another tip is to leave the dough underneath an upturned bowl for 5 minutes as this will soften it a little, making it easier to knead. Follow the step-by-step photographs on pages 34–35 (all the step-by-step sequences in the book follow this numbered pattern).

Combine the flour and fine semolina in a bowl, then tip onto a clean work surface or board and shape it into a mound. Make a well in the centre and crack the eggs into the middle.

Using a fork, break the eggs yolks and start to gently whisk them. Draw in the flour and semolina a little at a time and continue to combine together with the fork.

When everything starts to come together, use your hands to knead the dough for 8–10 minutes until smooth. Use the heel of one hand to push the dough away from you, and use your other hand to turn it 90 degrees after each knead – you will soon develop a lovely rhythm.

When the dough is smooth, form it into a flat disc (this will make it easier to roll out later). Place it in an airtight container in the fridge to rest for at least 30 minutes. Resting it makes the structure of the dough smoother and more pliable, so it's easier to roll out and shape. You can make the dough a day or two ahead, if preferred, as it will sit quite happily in the fridge for up to 48 hours.

Using a food processor

You can also make pasta dough in a food processor – it's really quick and easy, though I actually prefer to make it by hand, especially at home.

Place the flour and semolina in the processor bowl and secure the lid. Start the machine, then pour the eggs into the funnel.

Mix for 30 seconds, until the dough has the consistency of fine breadcrumbs.

Tip onto a board or into a bowl and use your hands to bring the mixture together to form a neat disc. Place the dough in an airtight container and refrigerate as opposite.

RICH EGG DOUGH

Makes 400g/14oz, enough to serve 4

280g/10oz Italian 00 flour

2 eggs, plus 4 egg yolks

I find that rich egg dough, made using additional egg yolks, creates a firmer, more pliable and more consistent dough. I'm exceptionally lucky to have access to such good eggs from St Ewe, a family farm more or less on my doorstep in southwest England. Their eggs have extra-rich yolks, vibrant and sunny, and they really make the pasta extra golden. If you can, hunt down eggs that are labelled rich-yolk, as they really do make a difference to the colour of your pasta.

Follow the classic dough recipe opposite. You can make it by hand or in the food processor.

CLASSIC PASTA DOUGHS

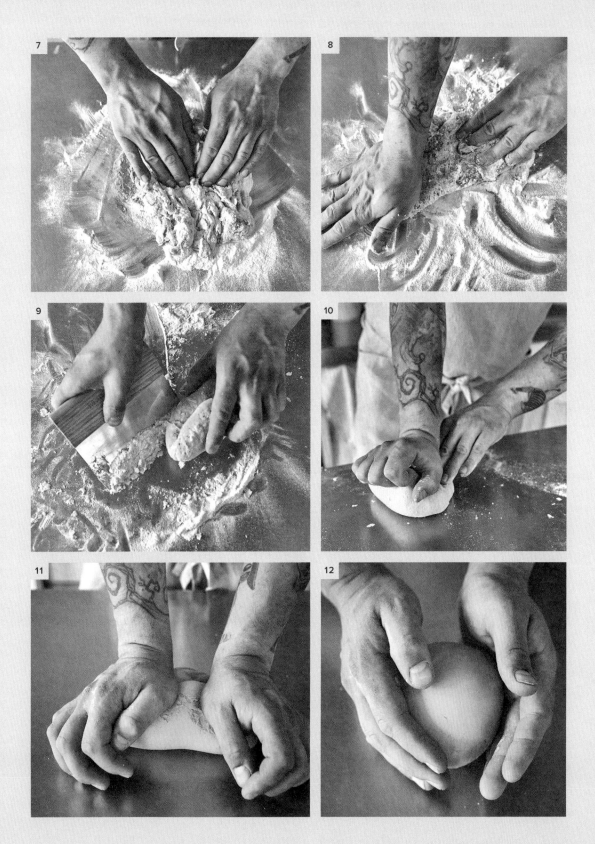

WHOLEMEAL EGG DOUGH

**Makes 400g/14oz,
enough to serve 4**

210g/7½oz Italian 00 flour

90g/3¼oz wholemeal
strong flour

3 eggs

It's always good to try to eat more whole grains, and the addition of strong wholemeal bread flour to 00 flour brings an extra nutty flavour to pasta. I've found that the best proportion is 30% wholemeal to 70% 00 flour, which creates a nice pliable dough that isn't too heavy. It can become very sticky as you roll it out, so if you find that happens, dust the dough generously with 00 flour as you progress through the settings on your pasta machine.

Follow the classic egg dough recipe on page 32. You can make it by hand or in the food processor.

CHESTNUT EGG DOUGH

**Makes 450g/1lb,
enough to serve 4**

255g/9 oz Italian 00 flour

90g/3¼oz chestnut flour

3 eggs

The smell of fresh chestnut dough is deliciously nutty and smoky, while the colour is a handsome beige-brown, which darkens and intensifies if the dough is left overnight in the fridge. Chestnut flour is rich in vitamins, protein and fibre, making it a very healthy addition to pasta dough. The flour is finely ground and gluten-free, but it needs to be mixed with standard 00 flour for the best results. I use it for its delicate colour and slightly sweet flavour, which pairs well with mushrooms, sausages and sage.

Follow the classic egg dough recipe on page 32. You can make it by hand or in the food processor.

EGG DOUGH WITH PARSLEY

**Makes 400g/14oz,
enough to serve 4**

3 eggs

½ bunch of parsley, leaves
picked and finely chopped
(about 15g/½oz)

300g/10½oz Italian 00 flour

It's fun to see this speckled dough rolling out of the pasta machine, and makes a change from classic egg pasta dough. It tends to work best in dishes where the herb complements the sauce, so for example, parsley works really well with a mushroom or creamy cheese sauce.

Break the eggs into a clean bowl, add the parsley and beat together with a fork until nicely mixed.

Place the flour on a clean work surface or board and shape it into a mound. Make a well in the centre and pour the egg mixture into the middle.

Using a fork, gently draw the flour into the eggs a little at a time and combine together. When the mixture is dry enough to work with your hands, knead the dough for 8–10 minutes until smooth. Use the heel of one hand to push the dough away from you, and use your other hand to turn it 90 degrees after each knead – you will soon develop a lovely rhythm.

When the dough is smooth, form it into a flat disc (this will make it easier to roll out later). Place it in an airtight container in the fridge to rest for at least 30 minutes. Resting it makes the structure of the dough smoother and more pliable, so it's easier to roll out and shape. You can make the dough a day or two ahead, if preferred, as it will sit quite happily wrapped in clingfilm (plastic wrap) in the fridge for up to 48 hours.

Using a food processor

Place the flour and chopped herbs in the processor bowl and secure the lid. Start the machine, then pour the eggs into the funnel.

Mix for 30 seconds, until the dough has the consistency of fine breadcrumbs.

Tip onto a board or into a bowl, and use your hands to bring the mixture together to form a neat disc.

Place the dough in an airtight container and refrigerate as above.

GLUTEN-FREE EGG DOUGH

Makes 400g/14oz, enough to serve 4

210g/7½oz chickpea (gram) flour

90g/3¼oz rice flour

3 eggs

Pasta is my favourite comfort food (a cheese toastie is a close second) and I can't imagine a life without it, so I've always been keen to find the best alternative recipe for people who are gluten intolerant. I'm happy to be able to offer this gluten-free recipe that is suitable for both ribbon and filled pastas. It's as close to a classic pasta dough as it could be, as the dough won't crumble when you shape it, even though it lacks the gluten to bind it, though you will still need to be careful when handling the dough as it is a little fragile.

Combine the flours in a bowl, then tip out onto a clean work surface or board and shape into a mound. Make a well in the centre and crack the eggs into the middle.

Using a fork, break the eggs yolks and start to gently whisk them. Draw in the flour a little at a time and continue to combine with the fork.

When everything starts to come together, use your hands to knead the dough for 3–5 minutes until smooth (the kneading time is shorter than for a classic dough as you're not developing the gluten here).

Place it in an airtight container in the fridge to rest for at least 30 minutes. You can make the dough a day or two ahead, if preferred, as it will sit quite happily in the fridge for up to 48 hours.

Using a food processor

This gluten-free dough takes so little kneading that it's probably just as quick to make by hand. However, if you prefer to use a food processor, place the flours in the processor bowl, secure the lid and start the machine, then pour the eggs into the funnel.

Mix for 30 seconds, until the dough has the consistency of fine breadcrumbs.

Tip onto a board or into a bowl, and use your hands to bring the mixture together to form a neat disc.

Place the dough in an airtight container and refrigerate as above.

VEGAN
SEMOLINA DOUGH

**Makes 400g/14oz,
enough to serve 4**

280g/10oz fine semolina

130ml/generous ½ cup
warm water

This eggless dough is made from *semolina rimacinata*, which means it is milled twice and helps to produce a fine-textured dough. You don't need a pasta machine to roll out this type of dough; it's usually used for shapes made using simple wooden tools or a knife, such as *trofie, orecchiette, malloreddus, busiate* or *foglie d'ulivo*.

When vegan semolina dough is cooked it has more bite than the softer egg pasta, and it also takes longer to cook – around 5–6 minutes instead of 2 minutes. It partners well with robust sauces such as *ragù* or *sugo*.

Place the semolina in a large mixing bowl, add a pinch of salt and pour in the warm water.

Combine with a fork – it will soon look like a crumble mix – and start to form the dough into a loose ball with your hands.

As soon as the dough has come together, turn it onto a clean work surface or board and knead until it is smooth and elastic – this will take about 10–15 minutes. Use the heel of one hand to push the dough away from you, and use your other hand to turn it 90 degrees after each knead – you will soon develop a lovely rhythm.

When the dough is smooth, form it into a flat disc (this will make it easier to roll out later). Place in an airtight container or under an upturned bowl to rest for 30 minutes, though you could actually use this vegan dough straightaway – it all depends how hungry you are.

Using a stand mixer

You can make this dough in a stand mixer with a dough hook attachment. Place the ingredients in the mixer bowl, start on a slow speed and mix steadily until the dough is formed. Tip onto a work surface, flatten into a disc and place in an airtight container or under an upturned bowl, as above.

EXTRUDED
SEMOLINA DOUGH

**Makes 400g/14oz,
enough to serve 4**

300g/10½oz fine semolina

about 100ml/scant ½ cup
water

At work we have a pasta extruder that's placed right by the window onto the street, and sometimes people stop to watch the pasta being fired out of the machine into a tray – *malloreddus*, *casarecce*, *mafaldine,* and more – it's hypnotic to watch. Children especially seem to like the theatre of the big window (and we like the theatre of watching them watching us). The domestic extruder I have at home is similarly hypnotic and always in use when we have a crowd to feed.

The principle is the same for both machines. Add the fine semolina to the chamber, switch on the mixer and slowly pour in the water. Hydration is between 32–35%, which means that each 100g/3½oz semolina needs to be mixed with 32–35g/1½oz water. The exact amount depends on the moisture in the atmosphere as well as how many batches of dough you make (when the machine becomes warm from use then the pasta requires a little less water to make).

First choose which shape you are going to make from the selection of bronze dies you have. Fasten the die in place (there is usually a small key to lock it in position). Add the semolina to the mixing chamber at the top of the machine, close the lid and switch it on to the mixing setting. Slowly pour the water through the safety grille; start by using 96g/scant 3½oz water, as you will need to check the consistency of the mixture before adding any more.

After 5 minutes of mixing, switch off the machine, lift the lid and scoop out a handful of the dough. Squeeze it in your hand – it will hold its shape – then release and try to crumble the mixture. If it crumbles into small pieces, it's ready to shape. If the mixture won't come together, you'll need to add a tiny bit more water and mix for a couple more minutes.

When you've checked that the texture is right, close the lid and switch on to the extruder setting. On my home machine I use a dough scraper to chop off the shape as it is squeezed through the die (if there's anyone else around they usually love volunteering for this task, though you do need to concentrate or you can end up with some wild-sized shapes!).

Spread out the extruded pasta shapes on the drying tray and set aside to dry out. If you're leaving it overnight, just cover it with a clean tea (dish) towel. When it's fully dried (this can take up to 12 hours), it can be stored in an airtight container – it looks pretty kept in a jar.

After you've finished using the machine, remove the parts that can be disassembled and wash them in warm soapy water. The machine itself must be wiped with a damp cloth (do not put it in water!). The bronze dies should be gently cleaned on the extruder side; I find it's best to use a toothpick to clean out any dough that's left behind. They should then be submerged in a small container of water and kept in the fridge, as this stops the bronze oxidising and discolouring in contact with air.

COLOURFUL
PASTA DOUGHS

I love being creative with colourful pasta doughs and I find it inspiring when I'm asked to produce something special or new for a particular event. My partner is a football fan and is always suggesting that I should make pasta in her team colours, but I've told her I draw the line at making blue pasta (if you'd like to do it, use pea flower powder).

Using natural powders – spirulina, activated charcoal, dehydrated vegetables – allows you to create a more consistent dough than using fresh produce such as spinach or beetroot (beets). I still like to make fresh vegetable doughs, but a dry powder mixed with the flour doesn't affect the moisture content in the way that the liquid in vegetables sometimes can.

Another bonus is that powders tend to produce more vibrant colours; you're never quite sure how dark a beetroot dough is going to turn out, but beetroot powder will give you the same result time after time. It's up to you, but if you're going to play with stripes or spirals then it's probably best to go for the powder method as it's much easier to make in small quantities.

Whichever method you choose, have fun playing with colour.

SPINACH EGG DOUGH

**Makes 400g/14oz,
enough to serve 4**

150g/5½oz spinach leaves,
washed

1 egg, plus 1 egg yolk

250g/9oz Italian 00 flour

If you like to eat your greens, why not make your carbs green too?
This is a classic recipe used to create a green-coloured pasta.
I like to make spinach *tagliatelle* to serve with a green vegetable
sauce – wild garlic pesto, soft slow-cooked courgettes (zucchini),
creamy gorgonzola and spinach – lovely, fresh springtime meals.

Bring a pan of water to the boil and blanch the spinach for
30–45 seconds, then tip into a colander to drain, and rinse
immediately under cold running water. When the spinach is cool
enough to handle, squeeze all of the moisture out of it (keep going
until there are no more drops of liquid – this is important).

Transfer the spinach to a blender with the whole egg, and blend until
it forms a loose purée – you should get about 100–110g/3½–4oz.

Mound the flour on a clean work surface or board and create a well
in the centre. Pour the spinach purée into the middle and add the
egg yolk. Start mixing the dough with a fork, drawing in a little bit of
flour at a time. When the dough starts to come together, knead it for
8–10 minutes until smooth. Use the heel of one hand to push the
dough away from you, and use your other hand to turn it 90 degrees
after each knead – you will soon develop a lovely rhythm.

When the dough is smooth, form it into a flat disc (this will make it
easier to roll out later). Place it in an airtight container in the fridge
to rest for at least 30 minutes. Resting it makes the structure of the
dough smoother and more pliable, so it's easier to roll out and shape.

Using a food processor

Make the spinach pureé as above, then transfer to a bowl, add the
extra egg yolk and beat gently together to combine.

Place the flour in the processor bowl and secure the lid. Start the
machine, then pour the spinach purée into the funnel.

Mix for 30 seconds until the dough has the consistency of fine
breadcrumbs.

Tip onto a board or into a bowl and use your hands to bring the
mixture together to form a neat disc. Place the dough in an airtight
container and refrigerate as above.

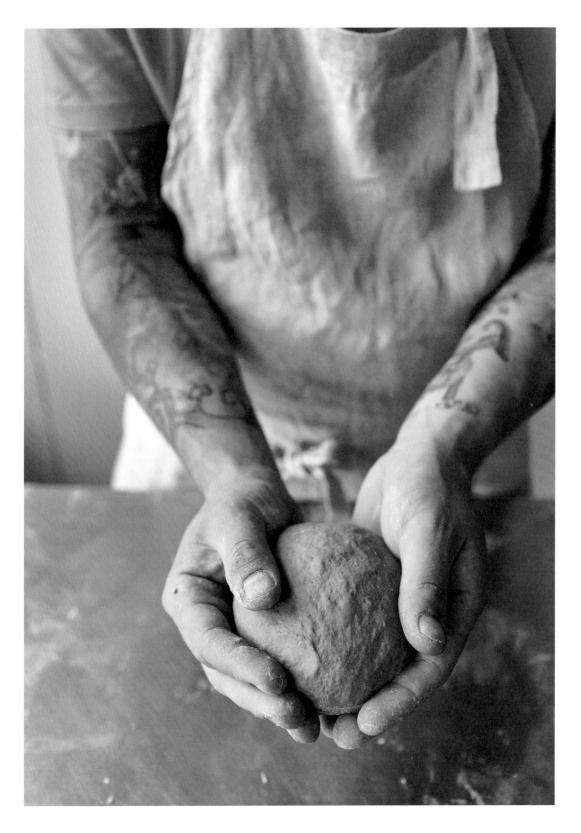

BEETROOT EGG DOUGH

**Make 400g/14oz,
enough to serve 4**

200g/7oz raw dark red
beetroot (beets), peeled and
chopped into small pieces

60g/2¼oz water

1 egg, plus 2 egg yolks

250g/9oz Italian 00 flour

I love eating *borscht*, so whenever I see beetroot (beets) at our local market, I come home with a couple of bunches to make this classic Eastern European soup. If I have a couple of roots to spare, I use them to make beetroot *cappelletti* or *tortellini* to go in the soup. You can also use this dough to play with stripy pasta, or make a mix of plain and colourful filled pasta shapes.

Put the beetroot (beets) into a blender and add the water, then blend to a purée. Add a little more water if you need to, but the key is to achieve a purée by adding as little liquid as possible.

Strain the purée through a sieve into a bowl, but don't press it – leave it to drip for 5 minutes. You will soon have a bowlful of bright red liquid.

Weigh out 40g/1½oz of the liquid into a bowl (the pulp left in the strainer can be added to the compost). Crack in the whole egg, add the 2 egg yolks and mix together with a fork.

Place the flour on a clean work surface or board, make a well in the centre, then add the egg and beetroot mixture in the middle. Start mixing the dough, using your fork to draw in a little bit of flour at a time.

When everything starts to come together, use your hands to knead the dough for 8–10 minutes until smooth. Use the heel of one hand to push the dough away from you, and use your other hand to turn it 90 degrees after each knead – you will soon develop a lovely rhythm.

When the dough is smooth, form it into a flat disc (this will make it easier to roll out later). Place it in an airtight container in the fridge to rest for at least 30 minutes. Resting it makes the structure of the dough smoother and more pliable, so it's easier to roll out and shape.

Using a food processor

Make the beetroot and egg mixture as above.

Place the flour in the processor bowl and secure the lid. Start the machine, then pour the beetroot and egg liquid into the funnel. Mix for 30 seconds, until the dough has the consistency of fine breadcrumbs.

Tip onto a board or into a bowl and use your hands to bring the mixture together to form a neat disc. Place the dough in an airtight container and refrigerate as above.

SQUID INK EGG DOUGH

**Makes 400g/14oz,
enough to serve 4**

2 eggs, plus 2 egg yolks

40g/1½oz squid ink

320g/11¼oz Italian 00 flour

If you'd like to make a black dough to eat with a fish-based pasta sauce, then this is the one to use, as it carries a strong flavour of the sea. You can buy squid ink at a good fishmonger, at a supermarket fish counter or at specialist online grocery stores.

If you'd like to use a black dough to experiment with creating stripes, I recommend using the charcoal dough instead (page 54). The method is more straightforward and you can make it in much smaller quantities, which is sometimes all you need.

Mix together the eggs, egg yolks and squid ink in a small bowl, making sure the whole mixture becomes black – you shouldn't see any streaks of yellow or orange yolk at all.

Place the flour on a clean work surface or board and pile it into a mound. Make a well in the centre and pour the egg and ink mixture into the middle. Using a fork, start drawing the flour into the egg and slowly mix.

When everything starts to come together, use your hands to knead the dough for a further 8–10 minutes until smooth. Use the heel of one hand to push the dough away from you, and use your other hand to turn it 90 degrees after each knead – you will soon develop a lovely rhythm.

When the dough is smooth, form it into a flat disc (this will make it easier to roll out later). Place it in an airtight container in the fridge to rest for at least 30 minutes. Resting it makes the structure of the dough smoother and more pliable, so it's easier to roll out and shape.

Using a food processor

Combine the eggs, egg yolks and squid ink as above.

Place the flour in the processor bowl and secure the lid. Start the machine, then pour the inky egg mixture into the funnel.

Mix for 30 seconds until the dough has the consistency of fine breadcrumbs.

Tip onto a board or into a bowl and use your hands to bring the mixture together to form a neat disc. Place the dough in an airtight container and refrigerate as above.

EGG DOUGH USING DEHYDRATED VEGETABLE POWDERS

Option One

Makes around 150g/5½oz dough, enough for 1, or to use for making patterns

70g/2½oz Italian 00 flour

30g/1oz fine semolina

1 tsp powder of your choice

1 egg

Option Two

Makes around 450g/1lb dough, enough for 4

210g/7½oz Italian 00 flour

90g/3¼oz fine semolina

3 tsp powder of your choice

3 eggs

It's much easier to make smaller batches of coloured doughs using dehydrated vegetable powders, which are flavourless and produce a good consistent colour. If you want to make multi-coloured pastas, then just make a small batch using Option One opposite (for the vegan version, see page 56). For a full batch of dough to serve four people, use the quantities of Option Two.

The method is very simple and essentially the same no matter what colour or quantity you make. Here are some of the most common powders you can use, which are readily available in supermarkets or online:

Activated charcoal – black

Beetroot (beets) – red

Cocoa – brown

Spirulina – dark green

Combine the flour, semolina and powder together in a bowl, then tip onto a clean work surface or board and pile it into a mound. Make a crater in the centre of the mound and drop in the egg(s).

Using a fork, start drawing the flour into the egg and slowly mix (this is where it's really exciting to see your colour develop).

When everything starts to come together, use your hands to knead the dough for a further 8–10 minutes until smooth. Use the heel of one hand to push the dough away from you, and use your other hand to turn it 90 degrees after each knead – you will soon develop a lovely rhythm.

When the dough is smooth, form it into a flat disc (this will make it easier to roll out later). Place it in an airtight container in the fridge to rest for at least 30 minutes. Resting it makes the structure of the dough smoother and more pliable, so it's easier to roll out and shape.

Using a food processor

Add the flour, semolina and powder to the processor bowl and secure the lid. Blitz for 10 seconds to combine.

Beat the eggs with a fork in a small bowl or jug, then pour into the funnel. Mix for 30 seconds, until the dough has the consistency of fine breadcrumbs.

Tip onto a board or into a bowl and bring the mixture together with your hands to form a neat disc.

Place the dough in an airtight container and refrigerate as above.

VEGAN DOUGH USING DEHYDRATED VEGETABLE POWDERS

Option One

Makes around 110g/4oz dough enough for 1, or to use for making patterns

75g/2¾oz fine semolina

½ tsp powder of
your choice

35g/1¼oz warm water

Option Two

Makes around 450g/1lb dough, enough for 4

300g/10½oz fine semolina

3 tsp powder
of your choice

135g/4¾oz warm water

As with the egg dough on the previous page, this method is very simple and is essentially the same no matter what colour or quantity you make. The warm water should be nearer tepid than hot – this simply makes it easier to knead the dough.

Place the semolina and powder in a large mixing bowl and pour the warm water all over them.

Combine with a fork – it will soon look like a crumble mix – then start to form the dough into a loose ball with your hands.

As soon as the dough has come together, turn it onto a clean work surface or board and knead until it is smooth and elastic – this will take about 10–15 minutes. Use the heel of one hand to push the dough away from you, and use your other hand to turn it 90 degrees after each knead – you will soon develop a lovely rhythm.

When the dough is smooth, form it into a flat disc (this will make it easier to roll out later). Place in an airtight container or under an upturned bowl to rest for 30 minutes, though you could actually use this vegan dough straight away – it all depends how hungry you are.

Using a stand mixer

Use a stand mixer with a dough hook attachment. Place all the ingredients in the mixer bowl, start on a slow speed and mix steadily until the dough is formed. Tip onto the work surface, flatten into a disc and place in an airtight container, as above.

Using a pasta extruder

Dissolve the coloured powder in the water before adding it to the extruder. Follow the steps on page 42 for full instructions on how to use the machine.

ROLLING &
SHAPING PASTA

Now for my favourite part of making pasta — the rolling and shaping. When I first started out it was a thrill just to make *tagliatelle*, but pasta-making is quite addictive, and the more your confidence grows and your technique improves, the more ambitious you can be. Even with quite complicated shapes, I always say just try; how wrong can it go?

At home I've always rolled pasta using a small pasta machine, but now I've got the space to try hand-rolling — *sfoglia* — and I'm really enjoying learning how to do it. I built a garden shed by watching videos on YouTube, and now I'm learning to hand-roll pasta by watching videos too (you can learn to be a car mechanic or a rocket scientist on YouTube these days!). One day I'd love to go for a lesson with a master *sfoglina* in Bologna, but until then I don't mind trying, making mistakes, improving, and eating the results enthusiastically no matter how imperfect they are. Always a good lesson in life.

A FEW NOTES ON ROLLING PASTA

The widest setting on my pasta machine is 0, so the settings I have used in this book are based on this. If your machine settings are reversed (i.e. if 0 is the thinnest setting), reverse the setting numbers accordingly throughout.

If you've made your dough a day ahead and stored it in the fridge, remember to take it out of the fridge 30 minutes before shaping. It's much easier to roll it at room temperature.

It's generally easiest to work with a quarter of the dough at a time (so, in 100g/3½oz portions). This prevents the dough drying out as you work, and you won't need to rush to finish rolling. Leave the rest of the dough in an airtight container or under a damp tea (dish) towel until you need it (just be careful the tea towel doesn't stick to your dough).

Always have some Italian 00 flour or fine semolina to hand when you are rolling as it's useful to dust the pasta with if the dough is a bit too soft.

Prepare a tray lightly dusted with coarse semolina, ready for your finished pasta shapes, and dust the pasta with more semolina as you lay it out. This prevents it sticking together.

Any leftover scraps of pasta after shaping can be cut into smaller pieces to use as *maltagliati* ('poorly cut' in Italian) (page 248). Freeze in a container or, if you prefer, freeze flat on a tray and transfer to a freezer container later; it's always nice to have some fresh pasta to throw into a soup to give it more body.

You can re-use any semolina that is left on the work surface when you lift off the pasta. Sieve it into a container and keep it for dusting the next time you're making pasta.

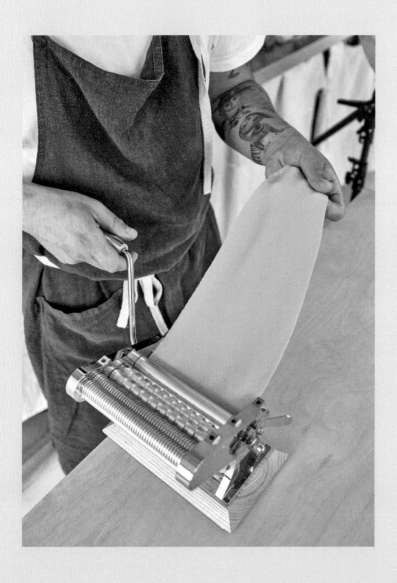

HOW TO ROLL PASTA DOUGH WITH A PASTA MACHINE

This is the rolling technique you'll need to refer to when you make most of the recipes in this book. Once you've done it a few times, it will become such a habit and you'll be so familiar with the settings on your machine that you won't need to re-read this. The machine setting for each pasta shape is included in the method, but do check back here if you're happier being guided step by step.

Cut roughly a quarter from your disc of pasta dough, then flatten it a little and guide it through the widest setting on your pasta machine twice (on my machine this is 0).

Move to the next widest setting (on my machine this is 1), then take the dough through this setting twice.

Now click back to the widest setting. Fold the dough in half from end to end, flatten it slightly and roll it through the machine twice.

Click to the next widest setting (you're now on 1 again). Roll the dough through the machine twice.

Continue to guide the dough twice through each setting. If you are making long ribbon pastas – *tagliatelle*, *tagliarini* or *pappardelle* – stop rolling at setting 6. If you are making filled pastas such as *ravioli*, *tortelli* or *caramelle*, you want the dough to be finer, so stop rolling on setting 7.

If the pasta dough is too sticky and proves difficult to roll out, gently dust it with 00 flour. Pat it lightly over the surface so that the dough *just* absorbs the flour, then you should be able to continue.

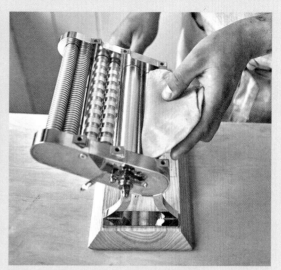
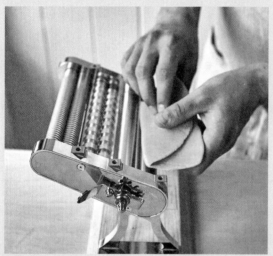

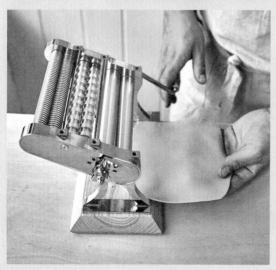

HOW TO ROLL
PASTA DOUGH WITH
A KITCHENAID

The pasta rolling attachment for a KitchenAid is an amazing invention. If you already have a KitchenAid, then the attachment is really worth considering as it makes it so easy to roll out sheets of dough, and it runs on different speeds to suit your level of experience. The attachment is a little narrower than a pasta machine, so try to roll the pasta as wide as will fit side to side. This is to make sure you don't waste dough when you are making filled pastas, or you'll end up having to re-roll the off-cuts.

Cut roughly a quarter from your disc of pasta dough, then flatten it a little and guide it through the widest setting (this is 1) twice.

Move to the next widest setting (this is 2), then take the dough through this setting twice.

Now click back to the widest setting. Fold the dough in half from end to end, flatten it slightly and turn it 90 degrees. Then roll it through the machine again twice. The reason for turning the dough is to create as wide a rectangle as possible.

Click to the next widest setting (you're now on 2 again). Roll the dough through the machine twice.

Continue to guide the dough twice through each setting. If you are making long ribbon pastas – *tagliatelle, tagliarini* or *pappardelle* – stop rolling at setting 5. If you are making filled pastas such as *ravioli, tortelli* or *caramelle*, you want the dough to be finer, so stop rolling on setting 6. If you like really thin, delicate pasta, then roll to setting 7.

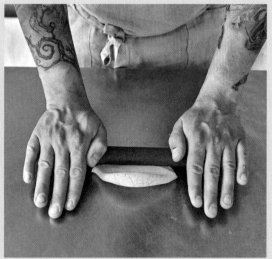

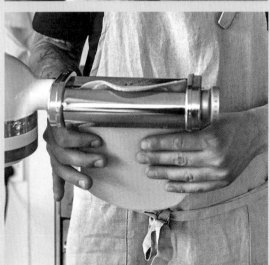

ROLLING MULTI-COLOURED PASTA

Learning how to make new pasta shapes is always exciting, but finding new ways of making multi-coloured pasta is like playtime. This is where I enjoy being creative – there are no rules and the sky's the limit. Stripes, spirals, patterns, pictures ... the only limits are your time, patience, and the colours you can make (I always use all-natural ingredients).

The front cover of my first book, *The Pasta Man*, features a picture of chequerboard pasta and was actually inspired by the Crittal windows in the photographer's studio, which had black metal frames. I was just playing around between shots, holding up the pasta to the window to catch the sun, and *boom!*, there was the cover shot. Since then, so many people have sent me pictures of their versions of this checked pasta, and I'm always really happy to see the book cover come to life.

When I'm making multi-coloured pastas, I usually start with a base of golden rich egg dough (page 33), then I choose other colours depending on which sauce or filling I'm using in the dish. Generally, the striped doughs are best used for filled pastas where you can really complement the shapes you make. If a recipe picture in this book shows colourful pasta, you don't have to make them this way; the recipes give you a quantity of dough and it's up to you if you want to make a colourful or multi-coloured dough instead.

So have fun, and I'll look forward to seeing your creations online!

TWO-SIDED STRIPES (METHOD 1)

200g/7oz classic or rich egg dough (pages 32 and 33)

200g/7oz any coloured egg dough (pages 44–54)

Take one quarter of the classic or rich egg dough (I recommend you weigh it carefully as you need exact quantities to create an even finish).

Flatten the dough to make it easier to start rolling. Roll the dough through the widest setting of your pasta machine (0 on mine). Roll it again through the same setting, tidying the edges to make an even rectangle. If the sides are still wavy, fold the dough lengthways and roll it again – each time you do this you'll achieve straighter edges.

When you have a neat rectangle, cover it with a tea (dish) towel or clingfilm (plastic wrap) and set it aside.

Repeat the above steps with a weighed quarter of the coloured dough.

Using a sharp knife, cut both doughs lengthways into 1cm/½in wide strips. Working quickly, spread out a sheet of baking parchment and lay alternate colours of dough side by side. The strips should just touch and not overlap – you will need to nudge them to lie snugly together. Roll back and forth with a rolling pin, pressing gently so that the edges of the strips connect to one another.

Slowly peel the pasta sheet off the baking parchment (it will be fragile until you've rolled it through the pasta machine). You may need to lift it from beneath with the blade of a large knife. Pass it carefully through the pasta machine on the second widest setting (on my machine this is 1).

Pass the dough twice more through each setting, finishing on setting 6 or 7, depending on how fine you want the dough to be. Repeat with the remaining dough. Trim the ends to make neat edges and you are ready to shape your pasta.

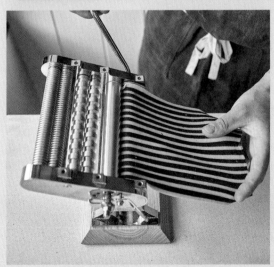

TWO-SIDED STRIPES (METHOD 2)

200g/7oz classic or rich egg dough (pages 32 and 33)

200g/7oz any coloured egg dough (pages 44–54)

Take one quarter of the classic or rich egg dough (I recommend you weigh it carefully as you need exact quantities to create an even finish).

Flatten the dough to make it easier to start rolling. Roll the dough through the widest setting of your pasta machine (0 on mine). Roll it again through the same setting, tidying the edges to make an even rectangle. If the sides are still wavy, fold the dough lengthways and roll it again – each time you do this you'll achieve straighter edges.

When you have a neat rectangle, cover it with a damp tea (dish) towel or clingfilm (plastic wrap) and set it aside.

Repeat the above steps with a weighed quarter of the coloured dough.

Lay the rectangle of coloured dough on top of the rectangle of plain dough. Roll over them a couple of times with a rolling pin to connect the two lightly together. Cut in half widthways, lift one of the halves and place it on top of the other one. Gently roll over with the rolling pin again, then cut in half and repeat this twice more. You will end up with a small rectangle of alternate-coloured layers (just like a stripy Liquorice Allsort).

Now use a sharp knife to slice the rectangle lengthways into 0.5–1cm/¼–½in strips (cutting along the bands of colour, not across them). Lay the strips side by side, just touching, on a sheet of baking parchment. Gently roll over them with the rolling pin to connect them, then feed the sheet through the widest setting of your pasta machine. Repeat, then continue to pass the dough twice through each setting, finishing on setting 6 or 7 depending on how fine you want the dough to be. Repeat with the remaining dough. Trim the ends to make neat edges and you are ready to shape your pasta.

ROLLING & SHAPING PASTA

ONE-SIDE-ONLY STRIPES AND PATTERNS

200g/7oz classic or rich egg dough (pages 32 and 33)

200g/7oz any coloured egg dough (pages 44–54)

This technique is really versatile as it simply involves connecting colourful dough to the egg dough using hand-cut shapes – simple stripes or more complex patterns – and then rolling them together. You can even use alphabet cutters to create a message in your pasta! The best part is that you can use any number of colours you like, especially if you have dehydrated vegetable powders and can make small batches of different colours.

Cut roughly one quarter from your disc of classic or rich egg dough, then flatten it a little and guide it twice through the widest setting on your pasta machine (0 on mine).

Move to the next widest setting, then roll the dough through it twice. Fold the dough in half from end to end, flatten it slightly and roll through the machine twice again on the widest setting, then guide the dough twice through each subsequent setting. For filled pasta such as *ravioli*, *caramelle* or *agnolini*, you want a fine, pliable dough, so stop rolling on setting 7. Lay out the pasta on a work surface and cover with a damp tea (dish) towel or clingfilm (plastic wrap).

Repeat the above process with a quarter of the coloured dough.

Lay the coloured sheet flat on the work surface and, using a sharp knife, cut strips of around 1cm/½in wide across the width of the dough. I use a metal ruler to keep the strips straight. Now arrange the coloured strips across the width of the egg dough sheet, laying them 1cm/½in apart for nice, even stripes, or play around with alternate thick or thin stripes, diagonals or chequerboard patterns. Some of the coloured strips may overhang the edges of the sheet of egg dough, so trim them to tidy up.

Using a rolling pin, roll gently over the whole sheet to connect the coloured strips to the egg dough sheet beneath.

Finally, guide the dough through the pasta machine again on setting 7, which will give you the finished sheet of dough. Repeat with the remaining dough, then you are ready to shape your pasta.

HERB-LAMINATED EGG DOUGH

400g/14oz classic or rich egg dough (pages 32 and 33)

handful of soft herbs and edible flower petals, picked

You can use any soft herbs or edible flowers to make this dough. Why not try flat-leaf parsley and borage flowers, or sprigs of dill and marigold petals? I tend to pair this pasta with light sauces so that the pretty dough is visible, so try it with butter sauces or make a filled pasta served in a clear broth.

Cut roughly one quarter from your disc of classic or rich egg dough, then flatten it a little and guide it twice through the widest setting on your pasta machine (0 on mine).

Move to the next widest setting, then roll the dough through it twice. Fold the dough in half from end to end, flatten it slightly and roll through the machine twice again on the widest setting, then guide the dough twice through each subsequent setting. For ribbon pastas, stop rolling at setting 6. For filled pastas such as *scarpinocc* or *sacchetti*, you want a fine, pliable dough, so stop rolling on setting 7.

Lay the pasta sheet flat on the work surface and gently fold it over to mark the centre of the sheet. Unfold the sheet and cut along the fold line. Arrange the leaves and flowers on one sheet; you can scatter them if you want a natural effect, but make sure they don't overlap. Lay the second sheet over the first and use a rolling pin to gently roll the two sheets together.

For ribbon pastas, roll the sheet through the pasta machine twice – once on setting 5, then on setting 6. I would recommend cutting the dough by hand to make *pappardelle* or *fettuccine* (if you use the pasta machine attachment, the blade can tear the dough when it encounters the leaves).

For filled pastas, roll the sheet through the pasta machine three times – once each on settings 5, 6 and 7 – then you are ready to shape. Repeat with the remaining dough.

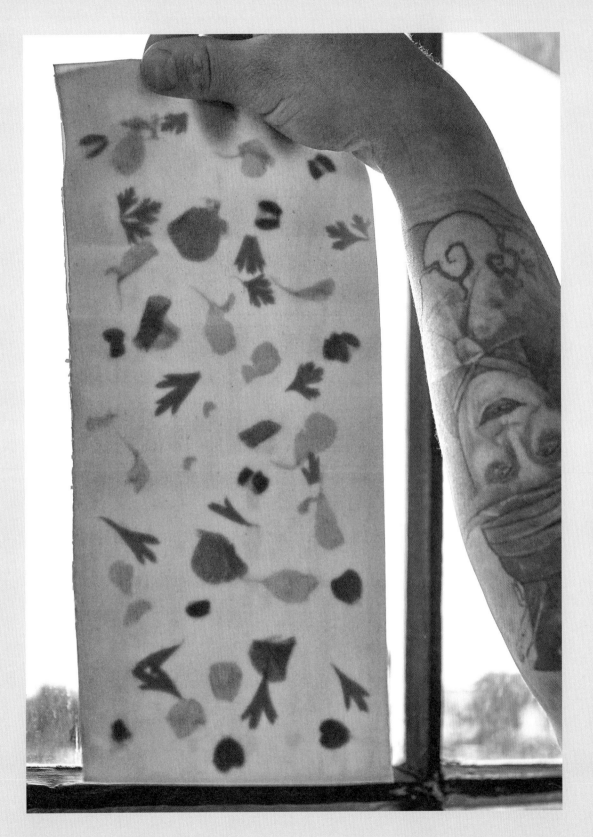

SHORT & RIBBON PASTA

FETTUCCINE, TAGLIATELLE, TAGLIARINI (THE THREE MUSKETEERS)

Equipment

pasta machine with cutter attachment

Everyone is familiar with these long ribbons of pasta; like spaghetti, they are all really popular shapes. I remember making *fettuccine* with my great-nieces Ella and Georgia. They were amazed when, having started with a messy pile of flour and eggs, we ended up with silky smooth sheets of pasta that fell from the cutter as skinny ribbons into their small hands. Served with a classic tomato sauce, dinner was soon on the table and, kids being kids, they got stuck in and ate it with their hands – no learning to twist the long strands of pasta around a fork, or not this time anyway. You can use any dough for this recipe but I usually use a classic egg dough (page 32).

Start with half the dough, leaving the other half in an airtight container, and prepare a tray dusted with coarse semolina.

Following the method on pages 60–65, roll out your pasta dough, stopping at setting 6, then cut the sheets into 25cm/10in lengths using a sharp kitchen knife.

Attach the pasta cutter to your machine and guide the sheets through on the relevant setting. Dust the cut pasta with semolina and either lay it flat on the tray (lift it by the centre of the strands and curl into individual nests) or hang it from a pasta drying rack. You don't need a rack, but it's fun to use – a wire or wooden coat hanger will do the job too. Repeat with the remaining dough.

Leave the pasta for about 30 minutes, so that it dries out slightly before cooking. If you are cutting the pasta more than an hour ahead of cooking, remember to cover the whole tray with a tea (dish) towel to keep it from drying out too much. If you are cutting the pasta a day ahead of cooking, dust it with semolina and store in an airtight container in the fridge.

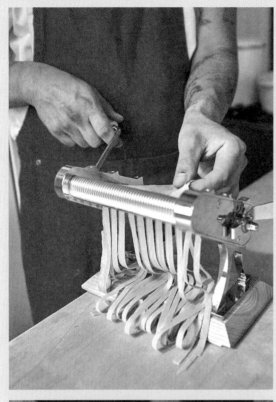

TAGLIATELLE WITH SALMON & CHERRY TOMATOES

Serves 4

400g/14oz *tagliatelle*
(page 78)

2 salmon fillets (around
400g/14oz)

60ml/4 tbsp olive oil

juice of 1 lemon

300g/10½oz cherry tomatoes,
halved

3 garlic cloves, sliced

bunch of parsley, leaves
picked and chopped

handful of mint leaves,
chopped

I like to make this dish when cherry tomatoes are in season,
as their sweetness contrasts so well with the herby lemon flavours
of the sauce.

Season the salmon by scattering sea salt on both sides of the fillets.

Warm 20ml/1½ tablespoons of olive oil in a frying pan (skillet) on
a medium-high heat. When you see the texture of the oil change
– it will appear thinner when it's hot – add the fish and reduce the
heat to medium. Fry for 4–5 minutes on each side until just cooked;
the fillets should still be soft and moist. Squeeze over half the
lemon juice and set aside to cool.

When the fish is cool enough to handle, flake the salmon, keeping
the pieces nice and chunky so that you have some bite in the sauce.

Heat the remaining olive oil in a large saucepan, then fry the
tomatoes for 2 minutes before adding the garlic. Cook for a further
2 minutes on a medium-low heat, then turn the heat right down
while you wait for the pasta to cook.

Bring a large pan of water to the boil, season generously with table
salt, and cook the *tagliatelle* for 1½–2 minutes.

Transfer the pasta into the tomato sauce using tongs. Add half
a ladleful of the pasta cooking water, along with the chopped herbs,
the remaining lemon juice and the flaked salmon. Toss it all together
so the sauce clings to the pasta ribbons. Season to taste with sea salt
and freshly ground black pepper.

Divide between four warm plates and serve with a glass of chilled
white wine for a perfect summer supper.

TAGLIARINI WITH CREAMY RICOTTA, LEMON AND SPINACH

Serves 4

400g/14oz *tagliarini* (page 78)

45ml/3 tbsp olive oil

2 garlic cloves, finely chopped

2 small shallots,
finely chopped

½ nutmeg

200g/7oz spinach leaves,
washed and chopped

350g/12oz ricotta

grated zest of 2 lemons,
plus juice of ½ lemon

45g/1½oz Parmesan,
finely grated

pangrattato (page 248),
to serve

Once, when I was talking to my friend Guiseppe in the kitchen, he told me that his mum often served him spaghetti with ricotta sauce when he was a kid, a fond childhood memory that made us both smile. In my version, I've added chopped spinach and nutmeg to give the sauce some body, and because I'm always looking for ways to add greens to a meal.

In a large saucepan, heat the olive oil and fry the garlic for 1 minute until fragrant, then add the shallots and cook on a medium-low heat for 5 minutes. Grate over the nutmeg and cook for a further 3 minutes to let the shallots absorb the aromatic flavour. Add the spinach along with 1 tablespoon of water, cover the pan with a lid and cook for a further 2 minutes until the spinach has wilted. Set aside to cool.

Combine the ricotta, lemon zest and Parmesan in a large bowl.

When the spinach is cool enough to handle, remove the excess liquid by squeezing it with your hands, then add it to the bowl of ricotta and combine everything together with a wooden spoon.

Bring a large pan of water to the boil and season generously with table salt. Take a ladleful of the boiling water and add it to the ricotta and spinach mixture, stirring it in to create a loose, creamy sauce. Now transfer this to a large saucepan and set it on a really low heat, keeping the sauce warm rather than cooking it.

Carefully drop the *tagliarini* into the boiling water and cook for 1½ minutes, then use tongs to lift the pasta into the sauce. Toss to mix it well. If the sauce is too thick, simply loosen it with more pasta cooking water. Squeeze over the juice of half a lemon and season to taste with sea salt and freshly ground black pepper.

Serve into four warmed bowls, with a generous sprinkling of *pangrattato* on top and a large dish of garlicky sautéed broccoli on the side.

TAGLIARINI
ALLA VONGOLE

Serves 4

400g/14oz *tagliarini*
(page 78)

800g/1lb 12oz clams (around
15 per person)

75ml/5 tbsp olive oil

4 garlic cloves, finely
chopped

120ml/½ cup white wine

3 red chillies, deseeded
and diced

juice of 1 lemon

½ bunch of parsley, leaves
picked and finely chopped
(or 100g/3½oz samphire,
trimmed)

A good fish-shop counter with an array of beautiful fish packed
in ice is a thing of joy, a window into another world beneath the sea.
I'd always recommend that you take the advice of an experienced
fishmonger when buying fresh fish. Clams are an altogether more
straightforward purchase; you simply buy them ready-packed
in bags of 800g/1lb 12oz or 1kg/2lb 4oz. If your fishmonger has
samphire for sale, then buy some to add to this dish too (you can
use it instead of the parsley).

Start by cleaning the clams. Soak them in a large bowl of cold
water for about 20 minutes, stirring to help release the grit. Drain,
then repeat the process three more times until the water looks clear.

Heat 45ml/3 tablespoons of the olive oil in a large saucepan on
a medium heat, add half of the garlic and fry for 2 minutes until
fragrant. Add the clams, turn up the heat to high, stir to cover the
shells with the hot oil, and quickly pour in the wine. Cover with a lid
and cook for a minute or two until all the clams are fully open.

Place a colander over a bowl and tip in the clams, allowing the liquid
to drain into the bowl. Set the liquid to one side. When the clams
are cool enough to handle, pick half of them, discarding the shells,
keeping the other half intact. Discard any that remain closed. Place
the picked meat and intact clams into a clean bowl.

Heat the remaining oil in a large saucepan and fry the rest of the
garlic along with the chillies for 2 minutes until fragrant. Add the clam
cooking liquid, then reduce the heat to low while the pasta cooks.

Bring a large pan of water to the boil and season generously with
table salt. If you're using samphire, now is the time to blanch it: boil
for 1 minute, then lift it out and set aside.

Drop the pasta into the boiling water and cook for 1½–2 minutes.
Use tongs to transfer the pasta to the saucepan of garlic and chilli.
Increase the heat to medium, toss everything together, then add the
clams and lemon juice and scatter over the parsley (or samphire).
Mix well and season to taste with sea salt and freshly ground pepper.

Serve into four warmed bowls and toast the bounty of the seashore
with a glass of chilled white wine.

FETTUCCINE CARBONARA

Serves 4

400g/14oz *fettuccine*
(page 78)

250g/9oz *guanciale*, cut into
small strips

1 egg, plus 3 egg yolks

60g/2¼oz pecorino, finely
grated, plus extra to serve

60g/2¼ oz Parmesan,
finely grated

juice of ½ lemon

Sometimes you stumble across the perfect place to eat at just
the right moment. This happened in Rome, when we had walked
too far and were beginning to feel very hungry. Cutting through
a back street somewhere near the Trevi Fountain, we came across
a small, busy restaurant with just one empty table outside, inviting
us to stop and eat. What a welcome plate of pasta carbonara that
was! You can serve this with classic spaghetti or with *rigatoni* if
you prefer.

Heat a large heavy-based frying pan on a medium-high heat, add
the *guanciale* and fry it for 6–8 minutes until golden and crispy.
Place a colander over a bowl and tip the *guanciale* into it. The fried
meat will retain its crispiness when separated from the fat, which
will drip through the colander. Pour the fat into a large saucepan
and set aside. Place the meat to one side too.

In a large bowl, beat the egg and egg yolks together with a wooden
spoon, then add the cheeses and plenty of freshly ground black
pepper (don't be shy). Beat again until you create a thick, grainy
paste. Set aside.

Bring a large pan of water to the boil, season it generously with
table salt and cook the *fettuccine* for 2 minutes.

Meanwhile, place the saucepan of fat over a low heat, add half
a ladleful of the pasta cooking water and swirl it together. Transfer
the cooked pasta into the fat using tongs, tossing together a few
times until the fatty liquid starts to coat the strands of pasta.

Now work quickly, as you need to avoid scrambling the eggs in the
hot pan. Take the saucepan off the heat and pour the egg mixture into
it, along with most of the *guanciale* (keep a little back as a garnish).
Mix really well, using either tongs or two spoons, lifting and turning
the strands of *fettuccine* to make sure they are well coated with the
sauce. Add the lemon juice and more pasta cooking water, if needed,
and season to taste with sea salt and freshly ground black pepper.

Divide the pasta among four plates, scatter the remaining crispy
guanciale over each one and serve with more pecorino (of course).

FETTUCCINE WITH VEGETARIAN 'NDUJA

Serves 4

400g/14oz *fettuccine*
(page 78)

5 Romano or Corno Rosso
peppers

50ml/3½ tbsp olive oil, plus
extra to drizzle

200g/7oz sundried tomatoes,
drained

10g/1/3oz cayenne pepper

8g/¼oz chilli flakes

10ml/¾ tbsp sherry vinegar

grated zest of 1 lemon

2 tbsp mascarpone cheese

bunch of parsley, leaves
picked and chopped

2 balls of *burrata*, halved,
or grated Parmesan, to serve
(optional)

Vegan options

Use *vegan semolina dough*
(page 41)

Replace the mascarpone with
oat crème fraîche

Serve with nutritional yeast
instead of the cheeses

Traditional Calabrian *'nduja* is made with fatty pork combined with herbs, spices and hot chillies, giving it quite a punch. Usually sold in jars or as a salami-style sausage in Italian delis, I love to eat it in toasties, melted with the butter of pan-fried white fish, dotted on top of a pizza, or served as a pasta sauce or filling.

This vegetarian version of an *'nduja* sauce can be used in a similar way; for a vegan version, omit the mascarpone and *burrata*.

Preheat the oven to 180°C fan/400°F/gas mark 6.

Place the whole red peppers onto a baking sheet lined with baking parchment, drizzle with olive oil and bake for 15–20 minutes until the skins are bubbled and brown. Remove from the oven, transfer to a bowl and cover with a plate or clingfilm (plastic wrap) until the peppers have steamed a little (this makes it easier to peel the skins). Once they are cool enough to handle, remove the stalks, slice in half to deseed, and remove the skins. Set aside.

Add the sundried tomatoes to the bowl of a food processor and blend for 30 seconds. Add the peppers, cayenne pepper and chilli flakes, turn on the food processor again and slowly pour the olive oil through the funnel in the lid. Once it's all incorporated, add the vinegar. When everything is nicely combined, add the lemon zest and mascarpone and mix once more. Season to taste with salt and black pepper and transfer the mixture to a large saucepan.

Bring a large pan of water to the boil before adding a generous amount of table salt. Carefully drop the pasta into the boiling water and cook for 2 minutes.

Meanwhile, heat the sauce, loosening it with half a ladleful of the pasta cooking water.

Using tongs, lift the cooked pasta into the saucepan (it's good to have some pasta water clinging to the ribbons of pasta). Add the chopped parsley, toss everything together to mix, and season to taste. If you need to add some extra water, now's the time.

Serve into four warmed bowls. I love having mine with half a creamy *burrata* on top, drizzled with olive oil and a sprinkling of freshly ground black pepper or a blizzard of Parmesan cheese.

SHORT & RIBBON PASTA

PAPPARDELLE

Equipment

pasta machine

kitchen knife

I really like to eat *pappardelle* with slow-cooked *ragù*; the sauce clings to the chunky ribbons of pasta, and every mouthful has a beautiful balance of flavour and texture. You can use any dough for this recipe but I usually use a classic egg dough (page 32).

Start with half the dough, leaving the other half in an airtight container, and prepare a tray dusted with coarse semolina.

Following the method on pages 60–65, roll out your dough to setting 6 on your pasta machine.

Cut the sheets into lengths using a sharp kitchen knife – I like mine around 15–20cm/6–8in long – then dust each sheet with semolina and stack them on top of one another. The aim is to produce a neat pile like a stack of playing cards.

When you've finished rolling the first half of the dough, gently fold the whole stack of sheets in half and turn the fold towards you.

Using a sharp knife, cut the sheets into ribbons about 3cm/1¼in wide.

Carefully lift each bundle of ribbons and gently shake off the semolina (some will still cling to the strands, but that's ok). Lay them in piles or folds on your tray, cover with a tea (dish) towel, and roll out the other half of the dough.

Leave the pasta for 30 minutes or so, so that it dries out slightly before cooking. If you are cutting the pasta more than an hour ahead of cooking, remember to cover the whole tray with a tea (dish) towel to stop it drying out too much. If you are shaping it a day ahead of cooking, turn each stack of *pappardelle* on to a cut side (which stops them from compacting), dust each one with semolina and store in an airtight container in the fridge.

PAPPARDELLE DUCK RAGÙ

Serves 4

400g/14oz *pappardelle*
(page 90)

60ml/4 tbsp olive oil,
plus extra to serve

2 medium shallots,
finely diced

2 garlic cloves, finely
chopped

1 medium carrot, diced

1 celery stick, diced

1 cinnamon stick

2 bay leaves

1 star anise

½ tsp ground ginger

2 tbsp agave syrup

3 duck legs

200ml/generous ¾ cup
red wine

bunch of parsley, leaves
picked and finely chopped

pecorino, to serve

Duck is not familiar to every home cook, but it's easy enough to find in grocery stores and is so simple to cook. The flavour of this dish reminds me of winter in Poland; at Christmastime we always had spiced duck served with crispy roast potatoes and a bowl of buttered cabbage. Here, duck with warm winter spices makes for a rich *ragù*, which hugs the fat ribbons of *pappardelle*. Dreamy.

Place a large saucepan on a medium heat, warm 45ml/3 tablespoons of the olive oil and fry the shallots, garlic, carrots and celery for 10 minutes to soften slightly. Place the cinnamon, bay leaves and star anise in a muslin (cheesecloth) spice bag, or tie them together with string, and add them to the saucepan along with the ground ginger and agave syrup. Cook the *soffritto* for a further 10 minutes, stirring occasionally, then take off the heat and leave to one side.

Preheat the oven to 170°C fan/375°F/gas mark 5.

Season the duck legs with sea salt and freshly ground pepper. Heat the remaining oil in a large frying pan (skillet) and sear the duck for about 5 minutes on each side. The duck will start to colour and crisp. Place the duck legs in a large casserole or ovenproof dish, together with the *soffritto* and spice bag. Pour in the red wine, then top up the liquid by adding just enough warm water to cover the duck. Cover with a lid (or tightly with a sheet of baking parchment, then with a sheet of foil). Place the casserole in the centre of the oven for 4 hours until the duck meat is falling off the bone. Set aside to cool a little.

Remove the duck legs from the casserole, along with the spice bag. When the duck is cool enough to handle, pull the meat from the bones and add it to the sauce, discarding the bones. Finely chop any large bits of skin and fat, then add these too. Mix everything together and season to taste with salt and pepper. Transfer the *ragù* to a large saucepan and place on a low heat while you cook the *pappardelle*.

Bring a large pan of water to the boil before seasoning with a generous amount of table salt. Drop in the *pappardelle* and cook it for 1½–2 minutes. Transfer the pasta to the ragù pan along with half a ladleful of pasta water, then turn up the heat to medium. Toss gently, scatter over the parsley then toss again, adding more pasta water if the sauce needs to be loosened. Serve into four warmed bowls and finish with a generous grating of pecorino.

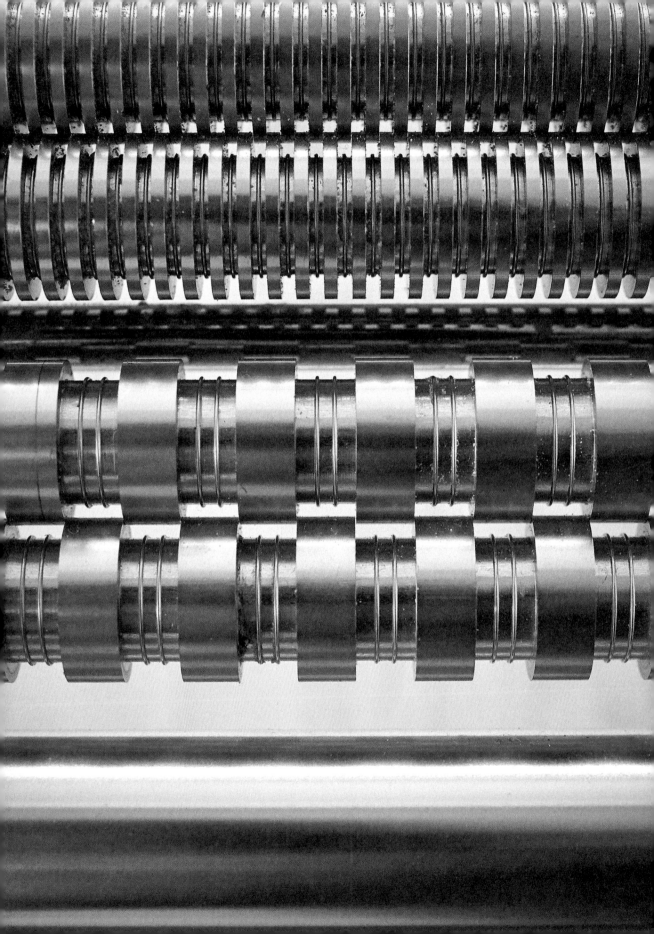

PICI

Equipment

kitchen knife

For the dough

350g/12oz strong white flour (or use Italian 00 flour, if preferred)

155g/5½oz water

20ml/1½ tbsp olive oil

pinch of table salt

This is a thick, hand-rolled pasta shape from Siena, Tuscany, a kind of fat spaghetti that's especially good for beginners as you don't need any special equipment. Usually made with plain or Italian 00 flour and water, sometimes with the addition of olive oil, it has a dense texture compared with egg pasta dough. I like to make it with strong bread flour, but why not try with whatever flour you have in your cupboard?

To make the dough, place all the ingredients in a large bowl. Combine with a fork, then start to form it into a loose ball with your hands. Turn onto a clean work surface or board and knead it until elastic and smooth. This will take about 10–15 minutes. Use the heel of one hand to push the dough away from you, and use your other hand to turn it 90 degrees after each knead.

You can also make this dough using a stand mixer with a dough hook attachment. Simply place the ingredients in the mixer bowl, start on a slow speed and mix steadily until the dough is formed.

Now form the dough into a flat disc (this will be much easier to roll out later). Wrap it tightly in clingfilm (plastic wrap) and rest in the fridge for at least 30 minutes.

Prepare a tray dusted with a generous amount of flour ready to lay out your pasta (use whatever flour you made your dough with).

Take a quarter of your dough, leaving the rest in the container until you're ready to use it. Slightly flatten the dough with your hand or a rolling pin to about 1cm/½in thick, then cut it into slim strips with a sharp kitchen knife.

Roll each strip into a rope the width of a slim pencil. It's easiest to roll from the middle outwards to get an even shape, but this is a rustic-style pasta so don't worry too much if it's a little lumpy and bumpy. Just make sure your work surface is clear of flour as this makes it difficult to roll the dough smoothly.

Place the finished *pici* flat on the prepared tray. When you have a handful ready, lift them together and swirl them in the flour on the tray to make sure they're well coated, adding more flour if necessary. Place each nest to one side of the work surface or on another floured tray while you continue to roll the remainder of the dough.

PICI ALLE BRICIOLE

Serves 4

one quantity of *pici* (page 96)

For the sauce

45ml/3 tbsp olive oil

3 garlic cloves, crushed

1 red chilli, deseeded
and diced

grated zest and juice of
½ lemon

small bunch of parsley, leaves
picked and chopped

80g/3oz *pangrattato*
(page 248)

pecorino or Parmesan,
to serve

Vegan option

Serve with nutritional yeast
instead of pecorino

A classic example of *cucina povera*, this Sienese dish is so simple yet full of flavour – just a few ingredients make a robust pasta that is tasty, filling and perfect after a day of hard work. Traditionally, *pici* is served with a rich *ragù* such as wild boar or duck, a rustic tomato sauce, or with creamy *cacio e pepe*, but I like this version. I think of this as an autumnal (fall) dish, something to eat after a long walk or a day spent working in the garden.

Bring a large pan of water to the boil before adding a generous amount of table salt. Cook the *pici* for 2–3 minutes.

At the same time, make the sauce. Heat the olive oil in a large saucepan and fry the garlic and chilli over a medium heat for 2 minutes. They will release their flavour into the oil but be careful not to let them brown or the garlic will become bitter.

Add half a ladleful of the pasta cooking water, then straightaway add the *pici*, using tongs to transfer them to the saucepan. Add the lemon juice and zest and toss together – the sauce will start to cling to the pasta. Add a touch more water, scatter over the parsley and *pangrattato* and mix everything well. Season to taste with sea salt and freshly ground black pepper.

Share between four warmed plates and finish with plenty of pecorino or Parmesan cheese.

CHITARRA

Equipment

pasta machine

chitarra box

The thin wire strings of the *chitarra* box are stretched across a wooden frame, similar to a guitar, which is where the name comes from. I love my *chitarra* box and can never resist playing on it, rock star style, before I actually start to cut pasta with it. The box I have now arrived as a surprise gift from an Instagram friend in the USA, R.J. Joyce, which is another reason I like it so much. That, and it makes me feel like Prince (the artist formerly known as) in the kitchen.

The cutter comes with a small rolling pin to push the pasta dough through the strings to make the shape known as *spaghetti alla chitarra*. The shape is, in fact, very similar to spaghetti, but with square strands instead of round.

You can make *chitarra* using egg or vegan dough, but I tend to use classic egg dough (page 32) as it's firmer and easier to work with.

Prepare a tray dusted with coarse semolina, and start with half the dough, leaving the rest in an airtight container.

Following the method on pages 60–65, roll out your pasta dough, stopping at setting 6.

If you're rolling by hand, aim for a rough square rather than a round shape as this will help you cut more even lengths of pasta and save you re-rolling too many off-cuts.

Cut the sheet into rectangles that are 5cm/2in shorter than the length of your *chitarra* box. Dust each sheet generously with semolina and stack them as you cut them.

Place a pasta sheet on top of the box along the line of the strings. Dust with more semolina and then, using the rolling pin, roll back and forth across the strings so that the strands fall through them into the box below.

Take out the *chitarra* strands and place them on the tray, either in straight lines or twisted into small nests. Dust with more semolina, cover with a cloth, and roll out the rest of your dough.

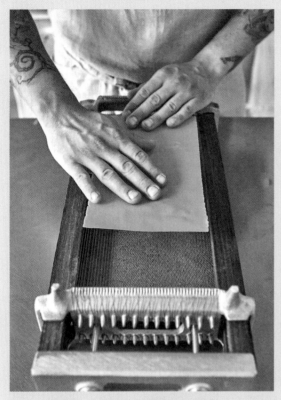
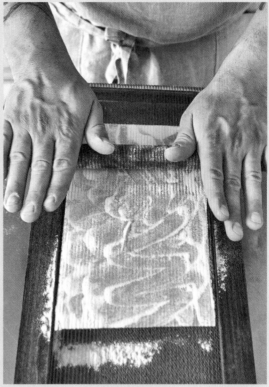

CHITARRA WITH COURGETTES, PEAS AND LEMON RICOTTA

Serves 4

400g/14oz *chitarra* (page 100)

For the sauce

400g courgettes (zucchini), coarsely grated

60ml/4 tbsp olive oil, plus a dash extra

3 garlic cloves, finely chopped

1 long red chilli, deseeded and finely chopped

80g/3oz frozen peas

3 sprigs of mint, leaves picked and roughly chopped

For the lemon ricotta

200g/7oz ricotta

grated zest and juice of 1 lemon

30ml/2 tbsp olive oil

30g/1oz Parmesan

I like to make this dish using a mix of green and yellow courgettes (zucchini), if there are any available. You don't really see much of the bold yellow colour once the courgettes are grated, but they have a mild buttery flavour which tastes of summer. The lemon ricotta adds a creamy sharp freshness to the dish (if you have any left over, it also goes well with butter tomato sauce, page 120).

Grate the courgettes (zucchini) using the largest holes on a box grater. Transfer to a colander, scatter with a generous pinch or two of table salt, mix well with your hands and leave to one side to allow the courgettes to lose some of their excess moisture. This will take about 30 minutes.

Next, make the lemon ricotta by combining all the ingredients in a medium bowl. Mix well with a wooden spoon and season to taste with sea salt and freshly ground black pepper. Cover and set aside while you make the courgette sauce.

Heat the olive oil in a large saucepan and fry the garlic and chilli for a couple of minutes until fragrant but not browned, then add the grated courgette and frozen peas and mix everything together. Leave on a low heat while you cook the pasta.

Set a large pan of water on the hob and, when the water is boiling, season it generously with table salt. Carefully drop the pasta into the water and cook for 2 minutes.

Use tongs to transfer the *chitarra* to the sauce, adding half a ladleful of the pasta cooking water. Add a dash of olive oil, scatter over the chopped mint leaves and toss together. Season to taste, then share between four warmed plates. Add a large spoonful of the lemony ricotta to each plate, finishing with a final twist of black pepper.

CHITARRA WITH SLOW-COOKED TOMATO SAUCE AND MEATBALLS

Serves 4

400g/14oz *chitarra* (page 100)

For the tomato sauce

60ml/4 tbsp olive oil

3 garlic cloves, finely chopped

2 x 400g/14oz cans of plum or chopped tomatoes

For the meatballs

400g/14oz minced (ground) pork

400g/14oz minced (ground) beef

100g/3½oz stale bread, toasted (or use the *pangrattato* on page 248, or Japanese panko breadcrumbs)

3 garlic cloves, peeled

2 medium shallots, peeled and roughly chopped

bunch of parsley

30g/1oz fresh green peppercorns in brine (optional)

1 egg

50g/2oz Parmesan, grated, plus extra to serve

1 tsp table salt

Vegetarian option

Use the meatless meatballs on page 247

This isn't a traditional Italian dish, but when your favourite TV programme is *The Sopranos* then you're always going to want to cook and eat Italian-American style, just like Tony did. I love food that can be shared by simply placing the cooking pot in the centre of the dinner table – easy-going, generous, convivial food.

The fresh green peppercorns are optional, but I urge you to buy a jar as they make the meatballs extra addictive.

For the tomato sauce, heat the olive oil in a large saucepan, add the garlic and fry for a minute until fragrant. Add the tomatoes, then cook on a low heat for 35–40 minutes, stirring occasionally. Set aside.

Meanwhile, place the toasted stale bread in the bowl of a food processor and whizz to fine breadcrumbs (don't worry about a few crusty chunks). Add the garlic, shallots, parsley and peppercorns and blend again to create a paste. Transfer this mixture to a bowl along with both meats, the egg, Parmesan and salt. Mix to combine.

Preheat the oven to 190°C fan/410°F/gas mark 6.

Now form your meatballs. Aim for the size of a whole walnut, but weigh the first one – it should be 25g/1oz – to give you about 40 small meatballs. Place them on a large baking sheet lined with baking parchment.

Bake the meatballs for 20 minutes, then drop them into the tomato sauce and set over a very low heat. (If you decide that 40 meatballs is too many, cool then freeze a dozen of them on a flat tray before transferring to a suitable container for use another time.)

Bring a large pan of water to the boil before adding a generous amount of table salt. Drop the pasta into the water and cook for 2 minutes. Transfer the *chitarra* to the pan of sauce using tongs. Gently mix everything together, adding a splash of pasta water to loosen if needed. Season to taste with sea salt and freshly ground black pepper.

Serve by placing the pot in the centre of the table along with a chunk of Parmesan, a fresh green salad and some cold beers.

SORPRESINE

Equipment

pasta machine

ruler

kitchen knife

Sorpresine is Italian for 'little surprises'. They look like little parcels, but then it turns out there's nothing inside them – not the best kind of surprise in my book. I love *sorpresine* anyway, especially cooked in a Parmesan broth. I often make this shape in autumn (fall), as you can add them to a nourishing, comforting minestrone or chicken broth when the weather turns cooler. You can use any dough for this recipe but I usually use a classic egg dough (page 32).

Start with a quarter of the dough, keeping the rest in an airtight container, and prepare a tray or baking sheet dusted with coarse semolina, on which to lay out your finished pasta.

Following the method on pages 60–65, roll out your pasta dough, stopping at setting 6.

Use a ruler and a kitchen knife to cut squares from the pasta sheet (if you have a multi-wheel cutter, this is a handy tool to use now). I like to cut squares around 3–4cm/1¼–1½in, as you will be able to spoon two or three at once from your broth – anything bigger is still nice but can overwhelm the soup.

Take a square, fold across from corner to corner and pinch the tip together to make a hollow triangle. Now pull the other two loose corners of the triangle down towards you – away from the top corner – and pinch them together. That's it.

Place your finished *sorpresine* on the dusted tray. There's no need to dust with more semolina, and you can leave them uncovered while you finish shaping the rest of the dough and make your broth.

SORPRESINE IN PARMESAN BROTH

Serves 4

400g/14oz *sorpresine*
(page 106)

1 small celeriac, peeled and
cut into small wedges

2 small carrots, peeled and
chopped into 3cm/1¼in pieces

2 medium onions,
cut into wedges

3 black peppercorns

½ bunch of parsley

3 garlic cloves, peeled

2 litres/4¼ US pints water

100g/3½oz Parmesan rind

Parmesan and green oil (page
249), to serve

Growing up in Poland, we always ate plenty of soups, invariably made with a chicken or beef stock. Nowadays I prefer to keep meat for special occasions, and at home I make vegetable broth as a base for soups. This *brodo* is a base recipe that I love to eat with *sorpresine*, *sfoglia lorda* or *tortellini*. The Parmesan rinds are added after the stock has cooked a little, otherwise its flavour can dominate the more delicate herbs and vegetables. Keep any leftover Parmesan rinds in a small box in the freezer; it's a good habit to reduce waste and get every last scrap of flavour from the cheese. You could also add leeks, parsnips or more herbs to the stock, or celeriac (celery root) leaves if you're lucky enough to have them; it just depends on what you have to hand in the kitchen.

First make the broth. Add all the ingredients except the Parmesan rind to a large pan, cover with cold water and bring to the boil. Simmer for 20 minutes, then add the Parmesan rind and continue to simmer for a further 25 minutes.

While the broth is simmering, shape the pasta and set to one side.

Carefully strain the liquid from the pan into another large pan, discard the vegetables, return the broth to the heat and allow to simmer for another 10 minutes. It will reduce a little and become more intense in flavour. Season to taste with table salt and freshly ground black pepper.

Add the *sorpresine* and cook for 1½–2 minutes. I like to serve this from the table: just place the pan in the middle along with a chunk of Parmesan and some green sauce and let everyone help themselves.

CORZETTI

Equipment

pasta machine or *mattarello*
(pasta rolling pin)

corzetti stamp

Sometimes called *croxetti*, this deceptively simple shape originates from Liguria, northwest Italy, and has been made and eaten since the Middle Ages. Originally the embossed image on the pasta would have been made with a coin or stamped with the coats of arms of noble families. Nowadays you can buy stamps, but there are a few craftsmen left who carve the wood by hand.

The beechwood *corzetti* stamp comes in two parts: a base cutter to cut out the circles of dough, and a handled top part, each carved with a pattern and which, when fitted together, emboss the dough on both sides. My favourite stamp has a bee motif on one side and a honeycomb on the other, but there are so many patterns to choose from, it's hard not to want them all.

You can use either egg or semolina dough for this shape, but I prefer to use vegan semolina dough, which is a little more pliable to work with and still embosses well.

Start with a quarter of the dough, keeping the rest in an airtight container, and prepare a tray or baking sheet dusted with coarse semolina, on which to lay out your finished pasta.

Roll out your dough following the method on pages 60–65 and roll to setting 5. The dough needs to have a little thickness to allow for imprinting the pattern on both sides. I like to practise rolling out the dough with a *mattarello*, a pasta rolling pin. It can be a little challenging to evenly roll out pasta dough by hand, but it's always worth having a go, especially when you're not aiming for a perfect shape. Aim for a sheet around 3mm/⅒ in thick.

Once you've rolled your dough, dust it with semolina on both sides and then, using the base of the *corzetti* stamp, gently twist it to cut out as many circles as you can from your sheet.

Now the fun part. Place a disc of dough on the stamp, pattern face up, then gently push the top down to sandwich the dough and apply just enough pressure to emboss it. I kind of wiggle it a little, but obviously don't twist the handle or you'll spoil the pattern. Gently remove and place the stamped pasta on the dusted tray. Repeat until you have a lovely pile of medallions. The scraps of leftover dough can be balled together and re-rolled to give a fresh and smooth sheet to work with.

CORZETTI SALSA DI NOCI

Serves 4

400g/14oz *corzetti* (page 110)

100g/3½ oz walnuts

2 slices of soft bread,
torn into pieces

175ml (scant ¾ cup) milk

2 garlic cloves

juice of ½ lemon

45ml/3 tbsp olive oil

50g/2oz Parmesan,
finely grated

I spent a very happy morning in the workshop of Filippo Romagnoli, a third-generation artisan woodcarver who lives and works outside Florence. His grandfather Ferrando was sent to be a cabinet-maker's apprentice at age 11 and started his own family business in 1918. Filippo now specialises in making pasta tools: beautiful rolling pins turned from Tuscan beech, walnut, lemon wood or mahogany, and dozens of different *corzetti* stamps, many of them made to commissioned designs. His workshop is like a small theatre, with Filippo centre stage bent over the woodturning machine, bringing precision and passion to every step of his work. It was Filippo who told me about this walnut sauce, and whenever I make it, I'm reminded of his wood-scented den.

I like to make the pasta here with vegan semolina dough (page 41) or wholemeal egg dough (page 36).

Bring a small saucepan of water to the boil, add the walnuts and boil them for 5 minutes. Drain them straightaway and allow to cool.

Soak the bread in the milk, ensuring the bread is completely covered by the liquid. After 5 minutes, squeeze the bread and transfer it to the bowl of a food processor, keeping the remaining milk to one side.

Add the boiled walnuts, garlic, lemon juice, olive oil and Parmesan and start to blend. Slowly pour the milk through the funnel of the processor until the mixture starts to look like porridge – a thick, grainy paste. Transfer the sauce to a large clean saucepan and set aside until you're ready to cook the pasta.

Bring a large pan of water to the boil before seasoning with a generous amount of table salt. Drop in the *corzetti* and boil for 2 minutes. While they are cooking, scoop out a ladleful of the pasta cooking water and pour it into the sauce, which should now be set over a medium heat. Stir in the water to create a looser sauce and season to taste with sea salt and freshly ground black pepper. I like this sauce to be quite peppery, so don't be shy.

Drain the pasta, reserving a small jugful of the cooking water, and add the *corzetti* to the sauce. Stir together with a large spoon, add more of the pasta cooking water if needed. Check the seasoning and you are ready to serve.

ALFABETO

Equipment

pasta machine

small alphabet cutters

People always laugh at *alphabetti spaghetti*, but I have never forgotten eating cans of this kids' favourite when I lived in London for a few months at the age of nine. Sometimes I used to eat it cold as I couldn't wait for the spaghetti to heat up, which also meant I was way too impatient to spell out any words from the letters that tipped out of the can.

This is a great pasta to make with children, but I'd set aside a bit of time because while in theory it's easy-peasy, small fingers can sometimes make for a slow job in the kitchen. At the end of it you can make them eat their words – but beware, unlike cookie dough, there's no snacking as you cut out the shapes. You can use any dough for these.

Start with a quarter of the dough, keeping the rest in an airtight container, and prepare a tray or baking sheet dusted with coarse semolina, on which to lay out your finished pasta.

Following the method on pages 60–65, roll out your pasta dough, stopping at setting 6.

If you are making this with children, you may want to cut the first sheet of dough into two or more pieces to share out the letter shaping. Working on a lightly floured surface, simply cut out as many letters as you can from each sheet and place on the prepared tray.

Collect up the off-cuts of dough – there will be a lot – and set aside while you continue to roll out and cut the rest of the dough. Gather up all the off-cuts together and re-roll them in your pasta machine, stopping at setting 6. Now you're ready to make more letters.

Don't forget to cut extra 'A's so that you can spell out 'The Pasta Man' when you've finished.

Some ideas for easy, kid-friendly sauces:

Basil pesto: Place a large bunch of basil, 30g/1oz toasted pine nuts, 40g/1½oz Parmesan and the juice of ½ lemon in a food processor, then slowly pour 130ml/generous ½ cup olive oil through the funnel until everything is blitzed together.

Butter sage sauce: see page 228

Butter tomato sauce: see page 120

SPIZZULUS

Equipment

garganelli or *cavarola* board
(page 13)

dough scraper or knife

This shape reminds me of those chunky, twisted-hoop, *Pirates-of-the-Caribbean*-style gold earrings. This semolina pasta has roots in Sardinia and, served in a rich tomato sauce, it's a bit like a grown-up version of spaghetti hoops. More childhood memories... I make these with vegan semolina dough (page 41).

Start with a quarter of the dough, keeping the rest in an airtight container, and prepare a tray or baking sheet dusted with coarse semolina, on which to lay out your finished pasta.

Using both hands, roll out the dough on a work surface until you have a long rope about 1cm/½in in diameter – something a little thicker than a pencil. Cut the pasta rope into pieces about 7.5cm/3in in length.

Take a *garganelli* or *cavarola* board and place a piece of dough onto the board at a 45-degree angle (rolling at this angle allows you to use a longer piece of dough, which is what you need to form the hoop). Using a dough scraper or an ordinary table knife, press down lightly on the dough so that it wraps around the blade slightly, then push the scraper away from you across the board in one smooth motion. The pasta should form a ridged roll, like a little caterpillar (if you use green semolina dough it will definitely look like a caterpillar).

Now take the ends and connect them together by pinching them to form a teardrop shape. Set on the dusted tray and keep going until you've used up all of the dough.

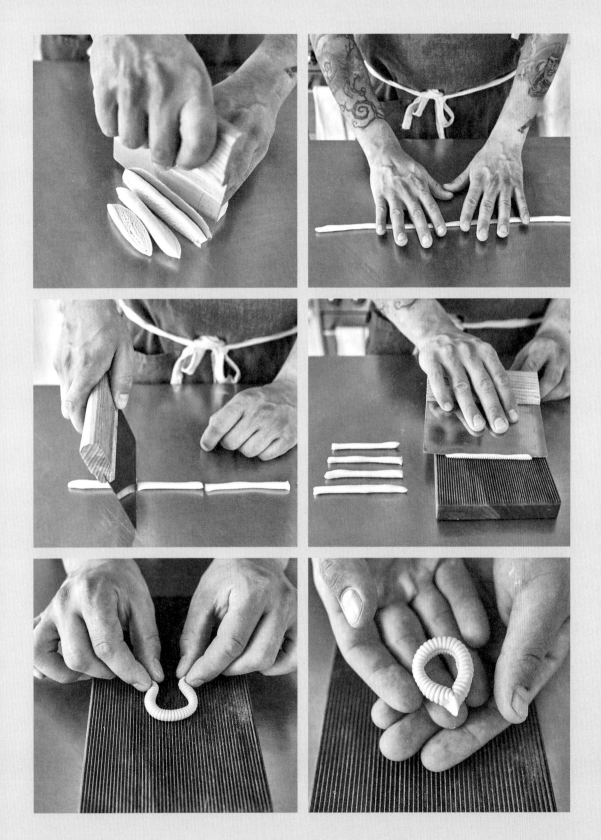

SPIZZULUS WITH
BUTTER TOMATO SAUCE

Serves 4

400g/14oz *spizzulus*
(page 118)

basil leaves (optional)

pecorino or Parmesan,
to serve

For the butter tomato sauce

60ml/4 tbsp olive oil

5 garlic cloves,
finely chopped

2 x 400g/14oz cans of plum
tomatoes or 600g/1lb 5oz
cherry tomatoes

1 tsp balsamic vinegar

60g/2¼oz butter, cubed

I love butter almost as much as pasta and I'm often accused of eating it like cheese. I'm always looking for ways to sneak it into my cooking, as so many things are improved by a little bit of butter. Here, it softens the sometimes sharp acidity of tomatoes, making this a particularly creamy tomato sauce. I've chosen to make the pasta here with the vegan spirulina dough (page 56).

Heat the olive oil in a large saucepan on a medium heat, then fry the garlic for a couple of minutes until fragrant but without letting it colour. Add the tomatoes (leave the cherry tomatoes whole if you're using fresh ones) and cook for 40 minutes on a medium-low heat, stirring occasionally. Half-cover the pan with a lid so that the tomatoes don't spit and splash as they bubble away.

At the end of the cooking time, break any tomatoes with the back of a wooden spoon if they haven't already split. Add the balsamic vinegar, then season to taste with sea salt and freshly ground black pepper. Leave the sauce on a low heat while you cook the pasta.

Bring a large pan of water to the boil before adding a generous amount of table salt, drop in the *spizzulus* and cook for 3–4 minutes. Drain the pasta, reserving some of the cooking water, and add the pasta to the sauce. Toss everything together, then stir in the butter until it melts. If you need to loosen it slightly, add a dash of the pasta cooking water.

Scatter over a handful of basil leaves, if you like, then serve straightaway with the cheese of your choice.

CAMPANELLE

Equipment

pasta machine

ravioli or pastry cutter

chopstick or thick skewer

Sometimes also called *gigli*, *campanelle* translates to 'bellflower' in English. Its delicate ruffled edges really do look like a pretty bell-shaped flower, and its hollow centre holds the sauce perfectly. We used to eat *campanelle* at home when I was a kid, served with creamy mushrooms and greens, one of my favourite family meals.

Usually made as an extruded pasta, you can also make it by hand, as I'm demonstrating here. It's quite slow-going, so it's a labour of love to make enough for a family supper. I'd recommend making just enough for a romantic meal for two instead. You can make this with any of the doughs but I favour making it with classic egg dough (page 32) or chestnut egg dough (page 36).

Start with a quarter of the dough, keeping the rest in an airtight container, and prepare a tray or baking sheet dusted with coarse semolina, on which to lay out your finished pasta.

Following the method on pages 60–65, roll out the dough to setting 6 on your pasta machine.

Lay the pasta sheet on a clean work surface and, using your *ravioli* cutter, cut rectangles roughly 3 x 4cm/1¼ x 1½in.

Take a rectangle, place the chopstick diagonally across one of the bottom corners, tuck the dough over the chopstick and start to roll it over. When you have completed the roll, curl back the top edges (a bit like peeling the wrapper back from a Cornetto ice cream) to create the bell shape. Slide out the stick and place the shape on the dusted tray.

Continue shaping until all the dough is used and you have enough for supper.

CAMPANELLE WITH MUSHROOM AND GORGONZOLA SAUCE

Serves 4

400g/14oz *campanelle*
(page 122)

90ml/6 tbsp olive oil

2 medium shallots,
finely diced

2 garlic cloves, finely diced

250g/9oz white or chestnut
mushrooms, sliced

3 celery sticks, chopped

140g/5½oz Gorgonzola dolce,
crumbled

80ml/5½ tbsp single cream

juice of ½ lemon

200g/7oz spinach leaves,
washed and chopped

Parmesan, to serve

Mushrooms, blue cheese, cream and spinach: a deliciously indulgent supper when good mushrooms are about. Paired with the delicate, nutty flavour of chestnut *campanelle*, this is a lovely autumnal (fall) dish. Use chestnut egg dough (page 36) to make the pasta here.

Heat 30ml/2 tablespoons olive oil in a large saucepan, add the shallots and garlic and cook for 7 minutes on a medium heat, stirring every couple of minutes until soft and slightly golden. Transfer to a clean bowl and leave to one side.

Using the same pan, add the remaining olive oil and fry the mushrooms and celery on a medium-high heat for 7–8 minutes, turning occasionally, until the mushrooms are cooked through and the celery retains some bite.

Reduce the heat to medium-low, add the Gorgonzola and allow it to slowly melt into the mushrooms, stirring gently to mix. Add the single cream and lemon juice, stir again to combine everything, then simmer for a couple of minutes. Add the chopped spinach to the pan, turn off the heat and set aside to allow the spinach to wilt into the sauce.

Set a large pan of water on the hob and, when the water is boiling, add plenty of table salt, then cook the *campanelle* for 2 minutes.

While the pasta is cooking, place the sauce back on a low heat, stir to combine the spinach, and season to taste with sea salt and freshly ground black pepper.

Drain the pasta, reserving a jugful of the pasta cooking water in case you need to loosen the sauce. Add the *campanelle* to the saucepan, toss everything together, taste again and you are ready to serve.

Share between four warmed bowls with a generous amount of Parmesan to grate over each one, and open a bottle of chilled dry white wine to drink alongside.

CAPPELLACCI
DEI BRIGANTI

Equipment

pasta machine

plain round cookie cutter
(about 7cm/2¾in)

People love the romance of the highwayman, with his dark cloak and black stallion – never mind that he's brandishing a loaded musket. Download Adam and the Ants to your playlist and make these brigands' hats to the sound of him singing 'Stand and deliver, your money or your life!' Rich egg dough (page 33) is my dough of choice for this shape.

Start with a quarter of the dough, keeping the rest in an airtight container, and prepare a tray or baking sheet dusted with coarse semolina, on which to lay out your finished pasta.

Following the method on pages 60–65, roll out the dough to setting 6 on your pasta machine.

Place the pasta sheet on a clean work surface and cut out circles using a cookie cutter (I use a 7cm/2¾in cutter, but don't worry if yours is a slightly different size). Keep all off-cuts well wrapped ready to use later.

Cut the circles in half and connect each one into a cone shape by folding the semicircle in half and pinching the straight edges together. Now turn up the brim of the hat, using your fingers. Alternatively, you can place the cone upside-down into the top of an empty wine bottle and fold the edges down over the lip of the bottle to create the brim.

Place the finished hats on the dusted tray and lightly dust with more semolina; they will need to dry a little to retain their shape.

Continue to roll and shape the remainder of the dough, including the off-cuts, which you can either re-roll or roughly cut to keep as *maltagliati* (they will keep in an airtight container for two days in the fridge, or you can freeze them for up to one month).

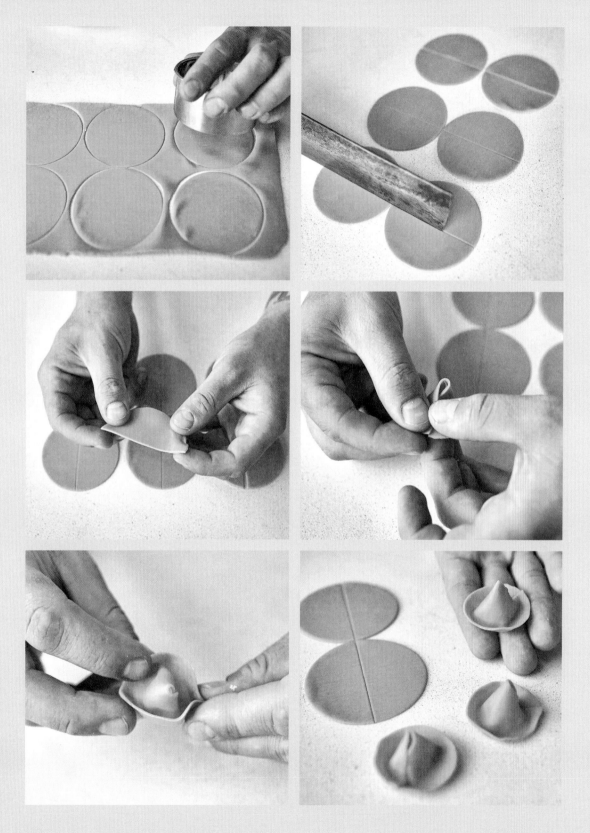

CAPPELLACCI DEI BRIGANTI WITH ARRABBIATA SAUCE

Serves 4

400g/14oz *cappellacci dei briganti* (page 126)

60ml/4 tbsp olive oil

4 garlic cloves, finely chopped

2 x 400g/14oz cans of whole plum tomatoes

1 tsp chilli flakes

basil leaves, to serve (optional)

pecorino, to serve

Vegan option

Use vegan *spizzulus* or *pici* instead of egg *cappellacci dei briganti*

Use nutritional yeast instead of the pecorino

Find yourself some good hot chilli flakes and the best canned tomatoes you can get – I like San Marzano or other whole plum tomatoes.

I've used rich egg dough (page 33) to make this pasta, but you can use a mix of beetroot (beets) and egg dough to create striped hats (200g/7oz of each dough). When you line them up to dry on the tray, they look a lot like mini traffic cones.

Heat the olive oil in a large saucepan, then add the garlic and fry on a medium heat until fragrant (a minute or two is enough) before adding the tomatoes. Continue to cook on a medium-low heat for 25 minutes, stirring occasionally. Add the chilli flakes and cook for a further 5 minutes. Take the pan off the heat and leave to one side while you prepare to cook the pasta.

Set a large pan filled with water on the hob and, when the water is boiling, season it generously with table salt. While you're waiting for the water to boil, set the sauce back on a low heat.

Add the pasta to the boiling water and cook for 2 minutes. Use a slotted spoon to transfer the *cappellacci* into the sauce, then mix well together so that the sauce coats the pasta and fills each little hat, adding a little pasta cooking water, if needed.

Share between four warmed plates, scatter with a few basil leaves if you like, and serve with a chunk of pecorino so that everyone can grate over as much cheese as they like.

PASSATELLI

Equipment

passatelli-maker
or potato ricer

When I met my friend Meri for Sunday lunch near Ferrara,
I wondered where we were going because the road petered out
into a country track and the car bumped along between the fields.
Eventually we arrived at a buzzing, crowded trattoria where a
christening celebration was taking place at one end and a birthday
party at the other. There wasn't a printed menu, the waitress simply
listed the types of pasta dishes available – over 30! – so of course
we had to try as many as we could.

The pastas arrived at our table in the pan, one after another, ready
for us to help ourselves: *triangoli*, *mezzelune*, *ravioli*, *pici*, *tortelli*,
tagliatelle, *chitarra*, all with deliciously different sauces and fillings.
We gave in at seven.

After this fantastically memorable lunch, we went back to Meri's
where, instead of taking an afternoon nap (which I was very much
tempted to do), we made more pasta. This is how I learned to make
passatelli, an unusual pasta made from breadcrumbs, Parmesan
and egg, then cooked directly *in brodo*. Meri used a traditional
passatelli-maker given to her by her grandparents, but you can
simply use a potato ricer. If you have one with interchangeable
inserts, then use the one with the largest holes as *passatelli* is
quite fragile, so ideally it shouldn't be too thin or it will just break
apart. (Recipe overleaf.)

PASSATELLI IN BRODO

Serves 4

For the chicken broth

1 x quantity meat broth (made with chicken) (page 246)

1 x quantity Parmesan broth (page 108)

95g/3½oz breadcrumbs or *pangrattato* (page 448)

95g/3½oz Parmesan, finely grated

grated zest of 1 lemon

2 eggs

½ nutmeg, grated

Parmesan, to serve

You will need to make your broth first and have it ready for your *passatelli*.

Add all the *passatelli* ingredients to a medium bowl and mix well using your hands. The mixture will start to come together into a ball, at which point you can place it on the work surface and knead the dough for 5–6 minutes. It will be on the dry side, but that's ok, it doesn't really resemble classic pasta dough in any way. Set the dough aside to rest for 10 minutes.

Using about a fifth of the dough at a time, squeeze it through the potato ricer (mine uses a twist mechanism which makes the job really easy). The dough emerges as rather crumbly strands, so it's best not to handle them too much or they will break up. Continue until you've used up all the dough.

Bring the broth to a bubbling simmer, then use a dough scraper to transfer the *passatelli* into it (this avoids lifting them with your fingers and breaking them). After a couple of minutes, the *passatelli* start to float to the surface of the broth, which means you are ready to serve it into warmed bowls. Grate a generous amount of Parmesan over each bowl and tuck in.

FARFALLE

Equipment

pasta machine

ravioli cutter

kitchen knife

ferretto (or wooden skewer)

Whenever I make *farfalle*, I can't resist saying aloud: 'The name's Bond. James Bond.' It's the bow tie shape that does it. Sometimes I get carried away and change it to: 'The name's Man. Pasta Man.' (I've never worn a bow tie – not yet anyway – but I have eaten loads of *farfalle*.)

This is a fun shape to play with if you want to mix colourful doughs, and kids like to make them too (in my experience they call them butterflies, as who wears a bow tie these days? Anyway, hats off to the kids, as the word *farfalle* actually means 'butterfly' in English). You can use any dough for this shape, but here I've used rich egg dough (page 33).

Start with a quarter of the dough, keeping the rest in an airtight container, and prepare a tray or baking sheet dusted with coarse semolina, on which to lay out your finished pasta.

Following the method on pages 60–65, roll out your pasta dough, stopping at setting 6.

Cut across the pasta sheet using the *ravioli* cutter and spacing the cuts around 5cm/2in apart. Next, using a sharp kitchen knife, cut lengthways at the same spacing to create squares. The squares will have the classic zig-zag edges on two opposite sides and be straight-edged on the other two sides.

If you want to be clever and you have a drawerful of kitchen equipment, you could use a multi-wheel pastry cutter (a *bicicletta*) to cut these shapes – it's much quicker when you're making large quantities, but it won't give you the patterned edges that I think are much nicer.

Place a square on the work surface with the zigzags to each side and the straight edges top and bottom. Lay the *ferretto* or skewer horizontally across the square and then, using a finger and thumb, pinch the dough across and over the top of the skewer. The dough will stick to form the bow tie shape, then you can carefully remove the skewer by simply sliding it out.

Place the *farfalle* on the dusted tray and continue with the rest of the dough until you have a nice pile.

FARFALLE WITH ROASTED TOMATO SAUCE

Serves 4

200g/7oz rich egg dough
(page 33)

200g/7oz beetroot egg dough
or vegetable powder dough
(pages 50 and 54)

500g/1lb 2oz red and yellow
cherry tomatoes, halved

4 garlic cloves, peeled

45ml/3 tbsp olive oil

2 tsp balsamic vinegar

large handful of basil leaves

large handful of mint leaves

Parmesan, to serve

Vegan option

Replace the egg *farfalle* with
vegan *busiate* (page 138)

Use nutritional yeast or
pangrattato (page 248)
instead of Parmesan

When I was travelling in northern Italy, I visited Acetaia San Giacomo near Modena, where I spent a happy morning with Andrea, the owner, finding out how balsamic vinegar is made. The *acetaia* (vinegar cellar) was filled with dozens of barrels arranged in sets called *batteria*, the barrels becoming progressively smaller as the balsamic is aged. Each barrel was made of a different wood – oak, chestnut, cherry, mulberry, juniper – adding to the extraordinary layers of flavour in the vinegar. Andrea can't be old enough to have made his own 25-year-old balsamic, but as his father ran the business before him, he has spent his life steeped in the fragrance of the *acetaia* and is a true craftsman.

Just a couple of teaspoons of good balsamic vinegar add such a depth of flavour to roasted tomato sauce, but I save the golden label 25-year vintage to eat drizzled onto slices of the best Parmesan cheese.

Make your stripy dough (pages 66–71), then roll and shape your *farfalle* (page 134) and set on a semolina-dusted tray.

Preheat the oven to 180°C fan/400°F/gas mark 6.

Place the tomatoes in a shallow ovenproof dish, tuck in the garlic and drizzle with the olive oil and balsamic vinegar. Cover the dish with foil and bake for 25 minutes until the garlic is soft and the tomatoes have slumped into their oily juices. Gently mash the garlic into the tomatoes and then transfer everything to a large saucepan. Place on a very low heat to keep warm while you cook the pasta.

Drop the *farfalle* into a large pan of boiling salted water and cook for 2 minutes. Drain the pasta, reserving a jugful of the pasta cooking water in case you need to loosen the sauce.

Transfer the *farfalle* to the tomato sauce, scatter with the herbs and toss together. Season to taste with sea salt and freshly ground black pepper and serve with plenty of grated Parmesan and a glass of red wine.

BUSIATE

Equipment

kitchen knife or dough scraper

ferretto (or wooden skewer)

A *ferretto* is a slim brass rod, usually but not always square shaped, around 30cm/12in long and used to make a number of long pasta shapes – it's not absolutely vital to have one to make *busiate*, as a wooden skewer or slim knitting needle will do if you'd like to give it a go. *Busiate* is traditional to Calabria and Sicily, and shaped something like an old-fashioned curly telephone wire (I loved that Julia Child, in the TV series *Julia*, had a fantastically long telephone cord that stretched right across the kitchen, so she could tuck the phone under her ear, chat, and still keep whisking eggs. We're not aiming to make anything quite as long as that here, though).

This shape is made with vegan semolina dough (page 41).

Start with a quarter of the dough, keeping the rest in an airtight container, and prepare a tray or baking sheet dusted with coarse semolina, on which to lay out your finished pasta.

Using both hands, roll out the dough on a work surface until you have a long rope about the thickness of a pencil. Using a kitchen knife or your dough scraper, cut the rope into 10–12cm/4–5in lengths.

Place a piece of the dough at a 45-degree angle in front of you on the work surface. Position the *ferretto* parallel to you, about 1cm/½in from the bottom end of the dough, which will create a V shape, then wrap a little of the dough around the rod to get you started. Using both hands, simply roll and push the rod away from you until the piece of dough is coiled right around it. Place the flat of your hand over the coil and roll backwards and forwards a couple of times – this will firm up the shape and will also help you to slide out the rod easily so you can start on the next one.

It may take a bit of practice to get your rolling technique right, but it's fun to learn and even more fun to eat the finished result, no matter how imperfect they might be to start with!

Keep going until your tray is filled and all of the dough is used up.

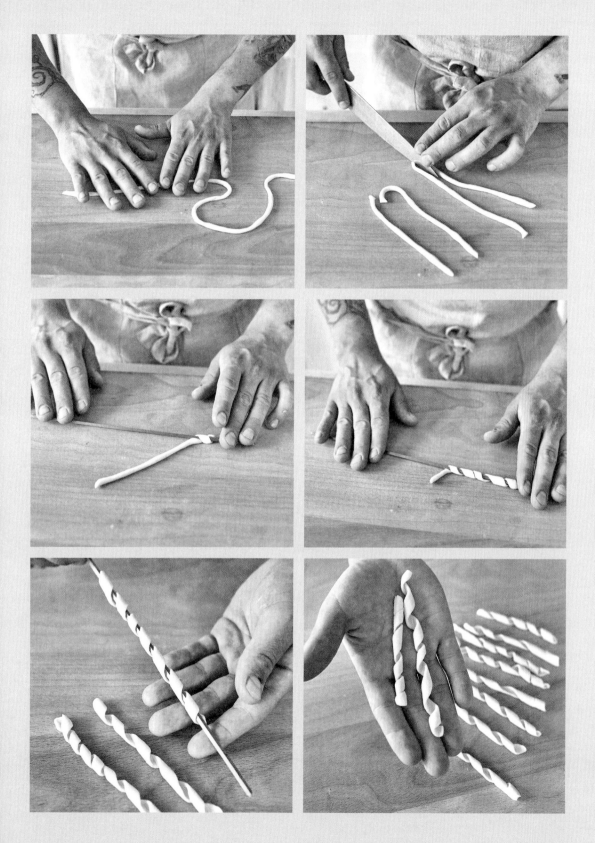

BUSIATE WITH TRAPANESE PESTO

Serves 4

400g/14oz *busiate* (page 138)

350g/12oz fresh San Marzano tomatoes (or any good plum tomatoes)

80g/3oz blanched whole almonds (or use skin-on if you prefer)

105ml/7 tbsp olive oil

2 garlic cloves, slightly crushed

juice of ½ lemon

4 stalks of basil, leaves only

2 stalks of mint, leaves only

60g/2¼oz pecorino, plus extra to serve

Vegan option

Replace the pecorino with *pangrattato*

There's always plenty of lively conversation when you work in a kitchen. Everyone loves to share food stories, favourite foods, to debate what's traditional and what's not. When I met Francesco, who comes from Puglia, he told me about his mum making *orecchiette* and *busiate* like a machine – she was so efficient and fast! Back then I hadn't really made either of these shapes, so Francesco's mum decided I needed to learn. She sent me a *ferretto* and her *orecchiette* knife with instructions to practise. It's wonderful how food connects you to people you haven't even met.

First, prepare the tomatoes. Score a cross in the stalk ends with a sharp knife, place the tomatoes in a large bowl and cover them with boiling water. After 1 minute, drain, then transfer to another bowl filled with ice-cold water. It will now be very easy to peel the skins, which can be discarded. Set the peeled tomatoes aside.

Place a frying pan (skillet) on a medium heat and toast the almonds for 6–8 minutes, shaking the pan from time to time until the almonds are golden brown. Transfer them to the bowl of a food processor and allow to cool.

Using the same pan, heat the 30ml/2 tablespoons olive oil on a medium-low heat, add the garlic and fry it for a couple of minutes to soften the cloves and flavour the oil. Tip the oil and garlic into the processor bowl with the almonds. Add the lemon juice and herbs and pulse for 20 seconds until the almonds are crushed.

Now place the tomatoes into the processor bowl, switch on the food processor and slowly pour the remaining olive oil through the funnel to blend everything together to create a thick, slightly grainy sauce.

Transfer to a large saucepan, season to taste with sea salt and freshly ground black pepper, then set over a very low heat.

Bring a large pan of water to the boil before salting generously, then drop in the *busiate* and cook for 2–3 minutes. Transfer the pasta to the warm sauce. Toss everything together, adding a splash of pasta water if needed, then scatter over the pecorino and toss again.

Season with sea salt and freshly ground black pepper, then share between plates with extra pecorino and a bowl of greens on the side.

ORECCHIETTE

Equipment

serrated knife or a plain table knife

The concave shape of *orecchiette*, thin in the middle, thicker around the edges, looks exactly like the curl of an ear, which is how the name originated: the Italian word for 'ears' is *orecchie*. In Bari, where this pasta comes from, it would be served with the classic *cime di rapa*, perhaps with an anchovy thrown in, but *orecchiette* also pairs well with a sundried tomato pesto (page 162) or a broccoli sauce.

There's no disguising that this shape is tricky to master but, like most things in life, patience and practice pay off. It took me a while to get the hang of it, but once you've found the right angle and pressure of the knife, you're halfway there. Learn to use your index fingers to guide the shape and you've cracked it. I make this shape with vegan semolina dough (page 41).

Start with a quarter of the dough, keeping the rest in an airtight container, and prepare a tray or baking sheet dusted with coarse semolina, on which to lay out your finished pasta.

Using both hands, roll out the dough on a work surface until you have a long rope about 2cm/¾in in diameter – pretty much the width of your finger.

Using a serrated knife, or a plain one if you prefer – try both and see which works best for you – cut a piece of dough about 1.5cm/just over ½in long. Holding your knife at a 45-degree angle, drag the blade towards you across the surface of the dough, following along with both index fingers to guide the shape. You will end up with a curl of pasta which you can open out a little if it's too tight. It should resemble half an empty walnut shell, a bit bumpy and rough – just what you need to capture the delicious sauce.

Continue with the rest of the dough until you have a lovely mound of pasta. Good luck!

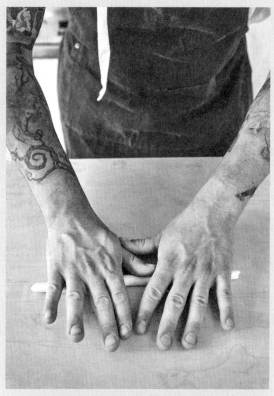

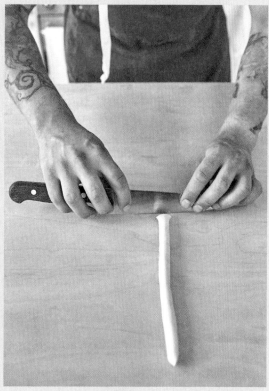

ORECCHIETTE WITH CIME DI RAPA

Serves 4

400g/14oz *orecchiette*
(page 142)

400g/14oz *cime di rapa*,
leaves only

45ml/3 tbsp olive oil

4 garlic cloves,
finely chopped

1 red chilli, diced, or
½ tsp red chilli flakes

6 anchovy fillets (optional)

juice of ½ lemon

pangrattato (page 248),
to serve

Vegan option

Omit the anchovies

Meat option

Replace the anchovies with
200–250g/7–9oz Italian
sausage meat. Fry the meat
in 1 tbsp of olive oil on a
medium-high heat until the
edges crisp up slightly, then
break it up with a wooden
spoon. Stir into the chilli and
garlic once they are cooked.

Cime di rapa (turnip tops, sometimes called broccoli rabe or rapini)
is very much a seasonal vegetable; you definitely won't see it in the
shops all year round, and you may have to go on the hunt for it.
If you haven't tried it before then you may be surprised by its rather
strong, bitter lemony flavour, but blanching it softens the bitterness
and it pairs really well with olive oil and chilli. Sausage meat is a
good addition to this sauce, and both options — with and without
the meat — are very common in Puglia.

Bring a medium-sized pan of water to the boil, season the water
with table salt and blanch the *cime di rapa* for 3 minutes, then
transfer immediately to ice-cold water (this helps to maintain the
colour of the leaves). Squeeze out the excess water and chop
roughly, then leave to one side.

Heat the olive oil in a large saucepan and fry the garlic and chilli on
a medium heat for a couple of minutes until fragrant but not coloured.
Add the anchovy fillets (if using) and cook on a low heat, stirring
occasionally, until the anchovies break up into the sauce. Leave on
a low heat while you cook the pasta.

Bring a large pan of water to the boil, season it generously with table
salt and cook the *orecchiette* for 2–3 minutes.

Meanwhile, add the *cime di rapa* to the saucepan of garlic and
anchovies, along with half a ladleful of the pasta cooking water.

Drain the cooked pasta, reserving a little of the cooking water,
then add the pasta to the sauce and toss together. Squeeze
the lemon juice into the pan and season to taste with sea salt
and freshly ground black pepper, adding more cooking water if
you need to.

Place the pan in the centre of the table (or transfer to a warmed bowl
if you prefer) along with a bowl of *pangrattato*, so everyone can help
themselves.

ORECCHIETTE WITH PISTACHIO PESTO, COURGETTES AND CHERRY TOMATOES

Serves 4

400g/14oz *orecchiette*
(page 142)

30ml/2 tbsp olive oil

250g/9oz Romana courgettes
(zucchini), cut into 1cm/½in rings

160g/5¾oz datterini or cherry
tomatoes, halved

pecorino or Parmesan, to serve

For the pistachio pesto

40g/1½oz shelled pistachios

bunch of basil (about 30g/1oz)

handful of mint

juice of 1 lemon

150g/5½oz olive oil

Vegan option

Serve with nutritional yeast or
pangrattato (page 248) instead
of pecorino or Parmesan

I absolutely love pistachios. Cracking them out of the shells to eat the roasted salted nut alongside an evening drink, baking ground pistachios in an olive oil cake with orange or lemon zest, blitzing them into a pesto to serve with pasta ... Pistachios give this recipe a Sicilian edge and add more body to the pesto than pine nuts. I like to use ribbed Romana courgettes (zucchini) if I can find them, as they have such a lovely texture and flavour, but ordinary courgettes will work.

Toast the pistachios in a dry frying pan (skillet) over a medium-low heat, shaking the pan from time to time until they are golden. This should take about 5–7 minutes.

Blitz the pistachios in a food processor, then add the basil and lemon juice. Pulse again and slowly add the olive oil through the funnel in the lid. You will end up with a dark green sauce with flecks of pistachio – how smooth you make it is up to you. Season to taste with sea salt and freshly ground black pepper, then transfer to a bowl and leave to one side.

Heat the 30ml/2 tablespoons olive oil in a large saucepan over a medium heat, add the courgettes (zucchini) and fry them until golden. You will need to turn them so that they cook evenly. Cover the pan with a lid and cook for a further 2 minutes – this will create steam inside the pan and will soften the courgettes.

Add the halved tomatoes and cook on a low heat for 5 minutes until the tomatoes have softened. Keep warm while you cook the *orecchiette*.

Bring a large pan of water to the boil, then season well with table salt. Drop in the pasta and cook for 2–3 minutes so that it retains some bite. Drain, reserving a jugful of pasta cooking water, and transfer the *orecchiette* to the pan of courgettes and tomatoes.

Now add the pesto and a generous splash of the pasta cooking water. Toss everything together well and check the seasoning before serving into warmed bowls. Finish each plate with finely grated pecorino or Parmesan.

SHORT & RIBBON PASTA

RIGATONI

Equipment

pasta machine

garganelli board

rolling pin (diameter 2cm/¾in)

Rigatoni is like *penne's* chunkier big brother, without the fancy angled ends. These ridged tubes are just asking to be covered in a rich tomato sauce and a blizzard of Parmesan. Often served with *carbonara* or *amatriciana* sauce, which clings to the rough surface of the pasta, it makes for a hearty autumnal (fall) supper.

Made commercially with an extruder, you can still make this shape by hand at home, though you will need a *garganelli* board to create the ridges (the name *rigatoni* comes from the Italian word *rigato*, meaning 'ridged'). You'll also need a rolling pin with a diameter of around 2cm/¾in. The small pin that comes with the *garganelli* board is too small to create this shape, an ordinary rolling pin too large, so you may need to improvise if you don't have the right-sized pin in your utensil drawer. Rich egg dough (page 33) is the perfect choice for this shape.

Start with a quarter of the dough, keeping the rest in an airtight container, and prepare a tray or baking sheet dusted with coarse semolina, on which to lay out your finished pasta.

Following the method on pages 60–65, roll out the dough to setting 5 on your pasta machine (the dough needs to be thicker for this pasta to hold its shape).

Cut out rectangles measuring 3 x 9cm/1¼ x 3½in.

Place the *garganelli* board horizontally in front of you on the work surface. Position a rectangle of dough across the ridges, place the rolling pin across the dough, then gently lift the bottom edge of the dough and wrap it over the pin. Now roll the whole thing across the ridges, applying more pressure over the join to make sure it connects properly and holds together.

Slide the *rigatoni* off the pin and place it upright on your dusted tray (if you lay them flat they will just sag and lose their round shape). The pasta will dry out slightly and you'll soon have a row of soldiers on parade as you work your way through the rest of the dough.

SHORT & RIBBON PASTA

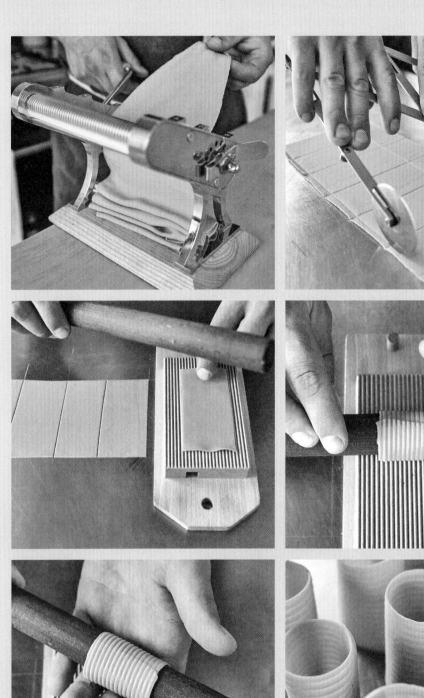

RIGATONI AMATRICIANA

Serves 4

400g/14oz *rigatoni* (page 148)

220g/7¾oz *guanciale*,
cut into small strips

3 garlic cloves, minced

2 x 400g/14oz cans
of plum tomatoes

120g/4¼oz pecorino, to serve

There are very few ingredients in this recipe, but the *guanciale* carries so much flavour, and cooking the tomatoes in its fat makes for a really flavourful sauce. Simplicity on a plate.

Heat a large heavy-based frying pan (skillet) on a medium-high heat, add the *guanciale* and fry it for 6–8 minutes until golden and crispy. Place a colander on top of a bowl and tip the *guanciale* into it. The fried meat will retain its crispiness when separated from the fat, which will drip through the colander and which can then be poured into a large saucepan. Place the meat to one side until you're ready to use it.

Re-heat the fat on a medium heat and fry the garlic for couple of minutes before adding the tomatoes. Bring to a bubbling simmer, half-cover with a lid and cook for 40–45 minutes, stirring occasionally. At the end of this time the sauce will have thickened and reduced. Now add three-quarters of the *guanciale* and leave on a low heat while you cook the pasta.

Bring a large pan of water to the boil and season it generously with table salt. Cook the *rigatoni* for 1½–2 minutes, then drain, reserving a jugful of the pasta cooking water. Add the *rigatoni* to the sauce, toss together and season to taste. I like my *amatriciana* to have a bit of a kick, so use a generous amount of freshly ground black pepper. Add more pasta cooking water, if needed, to loosen the sauce.

Divide between four warmed plates, scattering the remaining *guanciale* on top, and of course lots of pecorino too. *Bella.*

LORIGHITTAS

Equipment

just your hands

This Sardinian pasta is rarely made outside of the island. Why? I suppose some shapes just stay close to their geographical roots, especially if they can't be made commercially. *Lorighittas* were always made by hand and traditionally only by women; mothers would show their daughters how to make these special braids of pasta that look like twisted golden rings, possibly symbolic of a hoped-for wedding ring.

You don't need to sit out in the Sardinian sunshine with a reed basket ready to capture your finished *lorighittas*, though that does sound nice. I pass the time listening to music or a podcast while I twist the pasta ropes; it's a slow but soothing activity once you've got the hang of it. I make this shape with vegan semolina dough (page 41).

Start with a quarter of the dough, keeping the rest in an airtight container, and prepare a tray or baking sheet dusted with coarse semolina, on which to lay out your finished pasta.

Using both hands, roll out the dough on a work surface until you have a long, thin rope – aim for the width of a mobile phone charger cable. There's no need to worry about the exact length of the rope, as you'll nip off the end when you've coiled what you need.

Wrap the rope twice around three fingers of one hand then squeeze the dough together to connect the ends and nip off the excess.

Now the tricky part (which is where the QR code will help). Loosely hold the double circle of dough between the middle fingers and thumbs of both hands and gently twist the strands by simply rolling them between your fingers. Once it's completely twisted it's ready – place on the dusted sheet and continue until you've used up all the dough.

SHORT & RIBBON PASTA

LORIGHITTAS WITH LAMB AND SAFFRON RAGÙ

Serves 4

400g/14oz *lorighittas*
(page 152)

60ml/4 tbsp olive oil

1 onion, diced

4 garlic cloves, finely chopped

1 large carrot, diced

2 celery sticks, finely chopped

15 strands of saffron

200ml/generous ¾ cup
warm water

500g/1lb 2oz diced lamb

2 x 400g/14oz cans of whole
plum tomatoes

300ml/1¼ cups dry white wine

½ bunch parsley, leaves
picked and finely chopped

pecorino, finely grated,
to serve

Luca and I became friends when we both worked in Polpetto in London's Soho, and I went to stay with his family in Sardinia during the week of the *Sartiglia* carnival in February. His mum Francesca is a truly fantastic woman and all week she cooked so many special dishes for us – lamb shoulder *ragù*; lamb's trotters in tomato sauce; *seadas* (crisp pastries filled with pecorino and lemon zest served with honey); and of course lots of pasta. Luca now runs his own hotel in Sardinia, and when we talk on the phone the conversation always turns to food. This is a dish I hope to share with him the next time we meet.

First make a *soffritto*. Heat 45ml/3 tablespoons of the olive oil in a large saucepan and cook the onion, garlic, carrot and celery on a medium heat for 20 minutes, stirring occasionally, until the vegetables have softened a little and are just starting to caramelize.

Soak the saffron in the warm water and set aside for 10 minutes.

Meanwhile, sear the lamb. Heat the remaining olive oil in a large frying pan (skillet) and fry the diced lamb on a medium-high heat until the meat is nicely browned all over. This should take around 5 minutes. Transfer the meat to the *soffritto* and add the tomatoes, wine and saffron water.

Cover the saucepan with baking parchment – tuck it right down to rest on the surface of the sauce – then put the lid on the pan. Bring to a gentle boil, then turn the heat down and simmer the *ragù* for 2 hours. Check the meat has cooked through (you want the lamb to be really soft), then remove the pan from the heat and shred the meat using two forks. Stir the *ragù*, breaking up the tomatoes if any remain whole. Season to taste with sea salt and freshly ground black pepper.

Return the pan to a very low heat while you cook the pasta.

Bring a large pan of water to the boil before adding some table salt, then drop in the *lorighittas* and cook for 4–5 minutes. Drain the pasta, reserving a cupful of the pasta cooking water, and add the pasta to the *ragù*. Scatter over the parsley and mix everything together, then check the seasoning again. Add some pasta water if needed, but the *ragù* should be nicely moist and may not require any more liquid.

Ladle into four warmed bowls and serve with plenty of grated pecorino and a glass or two of good white wine.

SHORT & RIBBON PASTA

FOGLIE D'ULIVO

Equipment

table knife

dough scraper

The regions of Puglia and Liguria are renowned for their olive oil, and this shape is a tribute to their beautiful olive groves: *foglie d'ulivo* is Italian for 'olive leaves'. Sometimes spinach is added to the dough to mimic the colour of green leaves (page 48), but you can also use spirulina (pages 54 or 56), or make a mix of plain and green doughs.

This is another shape that involves rolling the dough into a rope, which is then cut and shaped with an ordinary table knife. If you use a knife that has some modest serration on the blade, you'll create a rougher surface which will help to catch and hold the sauce.

Start with a quarter of the dough, keeping the rest in an airtight container, and prepare a tray or baking sheet dusted with coarse semolina, on which to lay out your finished pasta.

Using your hands, start rolling the dough from the centre outwards to create a long rope about the thickness of a pencil – say 7mm/¼in. Cut the rope into three or four equal pieces, then line them up on the work surface in front of you to make it easy to cut across several at once. Cut them into lengths of 4cm/1½in using a dough scraper or the table knife.

Now take each piece in turn and roll them back and forth a couple of times across the work surface, or just pinch the ends between your finger and thumb; either method will slightly taper the ends to create a shape a bit like a small, plump pea pod. Place the knife parallel to the long edge of a piece of dough. Now press down and drag the knife across the dough, holding the edge of the dough with your fingers to stop it sliding and to stretch the dough into a leaf shape. Like making *orecchiette*, it's really about the texture of the dough and understanding how much pressure to apply. As always, a little practice goes a long way.

Continue with the remaining dough until you have a trayful of beautiful olive leaves.

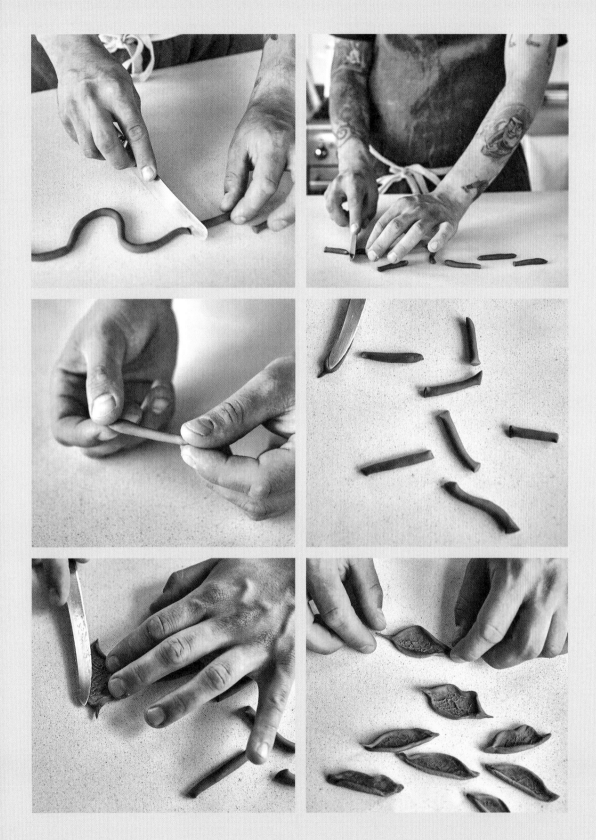

FOGLIE D'ULIVO WITH ANCHOVY PARSLEY PESTO

Serves 4

400g/14oz *foglie d'ulivo*
(page 156)

small head of broccoli,
cut into small pieces

80g/3oz parsley

2 garlic cloves

1 tsp sweet vinegar (sherry
or Moscatel)

130ml/generous ½ cup
olive oil

50g/2oz anchovies (use either
a jar or a can of fish)

juice of 1 lemon

pangrattato (page 248) or
nutritional yeast, to serve

Vegan option
Replace the anchovies with
a handful each of parsley, basil
and young spinach leaves, and
whizz together in the blender,
as above.

Anchoïade is a classic Provençal dip. I was making it to serve
with canapes for a party once, when I had the idea to simplify it
to create a pasta sauce. This is the result. The rich, dark green
of this pesto goes so well with this leaf-shaped pasta. If you like,
add extra herbs such as musky oregano, or a handful of mint leaves
to add freshness.

Blanch the broccoli by cooking it in boiling salted water for a couple
of minutes; it should be just tender and still bright green. Drain,
transfer the broccoli to a large saucepan and set aside.

Add the remaining ingredients to a blender jug and whizz everything
together until you create a lovely smooth green sauce (if you use
a food processor instead, the sauce will have the texture of a loose
pesto, but will taste just as good). Transfer to the pan containing the
broccoli and combine gently, then season to taste.

Set a large pan of water on the hob to boil before adding table salt.
Carefully drop the pasta into the boiling water and cook for 2 minutes.

Meanwhile, set the sauce on a medium heat. Take half a ladleful of
the pasta cooking water and add it to the saucepan to loosen the
mixture a little. Drain the pasta, reserving some more of the cooking
water in case you need it, then transfer the pasta into the sauce.
Gently mix with a spoon and season to taste with sea salt and freshly
ground black pepper.

Divide between four warm plates, and scatter over the *pangrattato* or
nutritional yeast. It's also good to serve up some chunks of bread to
fare la scarpetta – using torn bread to soak up any delicious sauce
left on the plate.

TROFIE

Equipment

just your hands

This little corkscrew of pasta comes from the region of Liguria in northern Italy, where it is perfectly paired with pesto alla Genovese, potatoes and green beans to make one of my favourite summer-time dishes.

Simply made with vegan semolina dough (page 41), the time it takes to make this pasta is mostly spent on shaping. It's another tricky one to master, but once you've got the hang of it, you'll soon speed up, and you can always pour yourself a glass of wine while you practise.

I much prefer to make this on a wooden board or work surface, as this helps to create some grip when rolling the pasta into spirals; a marble or other smooth work surface is a bit too slippy. The knack to making *trofie* is in using the outer edge of your palm to roll the spiral; angle it correctly and a lovely corkscrew emerges from beneath the padded side of your palm.

Start with a quarter of the vegan semolina dough, keeping the rest in an airtight container, and prepare a tray or baking sheet dusted with coarse semolina, on which to lay out your finished pasta.

Pinch off a thumbnail-sized piece of dough, roll it forwards with the flat of your hand, then, with your palm at a slight angle (about 40 degrees), roll the pasta back on the diagonal – this is what gives you the twist (definitely scan the QR code for this one as it's a little tricky to master!).

Lay the finished *trofie* on the prepared tray and dust with a little more semolina. Keep going until all the dough has gone.

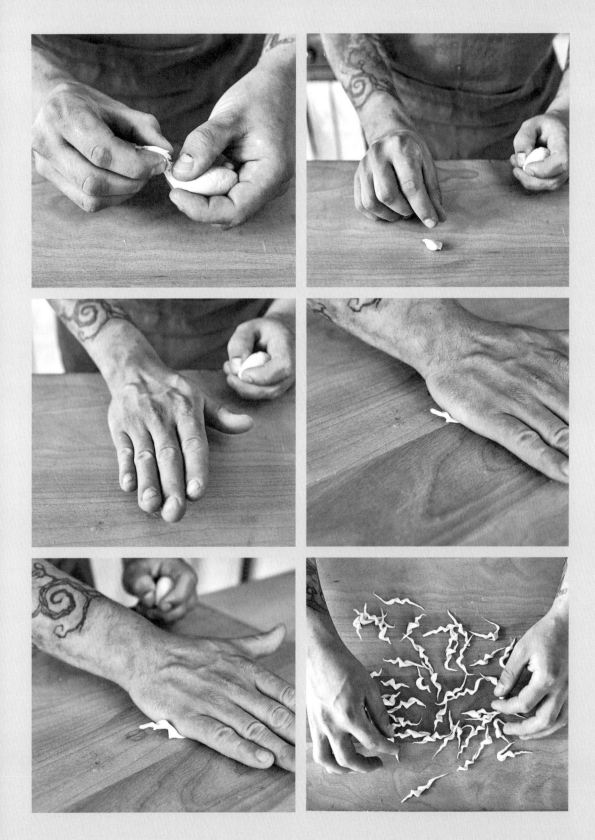

TROFIE WITH SUNDRIED TOMATO PESTO

Serves 4

400g/14oz *trofie* (page 160)

35g/1¼oz pine nuts

1 garlic clove, peeled

250g/9oz sundried tomatoes, drained

handful of basil leaves

juice of ½ lemon

100ml/7 tbsp olive oil

60g/2¼oz Parmesan, grated

Vegan option

Replace the Parmesan with *pangrattato* (page 248)

I have a rather romantic idea of sundried tomatoes – they conjure up a dream of the Italian south, where tomatoes are abundant, full of fragrance and flavour, and dried on wooden tables in the hot summer sun. (I expect the reality is more prosaic than that, but let's not spoil the dream.) It's so evocative to open a jar, even if you just bought it at the supermarket, especially in midwinter when you're longing for some summer warmth.

I recommend using tomatoes marinated in oil, but if you're using dried, don't forget to soak them in warm water for at least 2 hours before you make this pesto. I tend to use this sauce with eggless pasta as it is quite rich, but it also works really well as a sauce for classic *ravioli* filled with ricotta and spinach.

Toast the pine nuts by placing them in a small frying pan (skillet) on a medium heat until they start to turn golden. Keep an eye on them to make sure they don't burn (this can happen quickly if you turn your back for a moment, so best not to).

Transfer the toasted nuts to the bowl of a food processor and add the garlic, sundried tomatoes, most of the basil and the lemon juice. Blend for about 10–15 seconds, then add the olive oil by pouring it slowly through the funnel in the lid. Once everything is combined to a form a paste, use a spatula to scoop the pesto into a large saucepan. Set aside.

Bring a large pan of water to the boil before adding table salt, then drop in the *trofie*. Cook for 2–3 minutes, then drain the pasta, making sure you save a small jugful of the pasta cooking water. While the pasta is cooking, put the saucepan of pesto on a medium-low heat.

Transfer the *trofie* to the warmed pesto, add a generous splash of the pasta cooking water and toss together. Scatter the Parmesan over the pasta and mix until everything looks nicely coated, then scatter with the remaining basil. I like to serve this in a large bowl alongside a dressed green salad and let everyone help themselves.

FILLED PASTA & DUMPLINGS

MEZZELUNE

Equipment

pasta machine

cookie cutter (7.5cm/3in,
or bigger if you prefer)

piping bag (optional)

Mezzaluna is the Italian word for 'half-moon', which exactly describes this shape: a semi-circular pasta which can be filled with the classic ricotta and herbs, with Parmesan and potato, or with creamy pumpkin or garlicky mushrooms. Like *ravioli*, you can make them in many different sizes, and the method is pretty much the same. I like making them to a size that will give you a couple of mouthfuls from each parcel. I always like to cut a filled pasta to see what's inside; it feels like peeping inside the paper of a Christmas present.

If you use a fluted cookie cutter you'll create a pretty edge to the *mezzelune*, but a plain one will do the job just as well – it's up to you. I like to make this shape with classic egg dough (page 32) or herb-laminated egg dough (page 74).

As always, I suggest starting with a quarter of the dough, keeping the rest in an airtight container. Prepare a tray or baking sheet dusted with coarse semolina, on which to lay out your finished pasta.

Roll out the dough to setting 7 on your pasta machine (page 60). Lay the rolled sheet on a clean work surface and cut out as many circles as you can. Lift away the off-cuts of dough, squeeze them together and place with the rest of the dough to re-roll later on.

Using a piping bag or just a teaspoon, place a little filling in the centre of each circle, leaving a finger-width of plain dough around the edge. Lift up each piece, being careful to use both hands, then fold the edges across the centre to create a semi-circle. Press the edges together, pushing out any air bubbles as you go around.

Place each finished shape on your tray and continue filling and shaping until all the dough is used up.

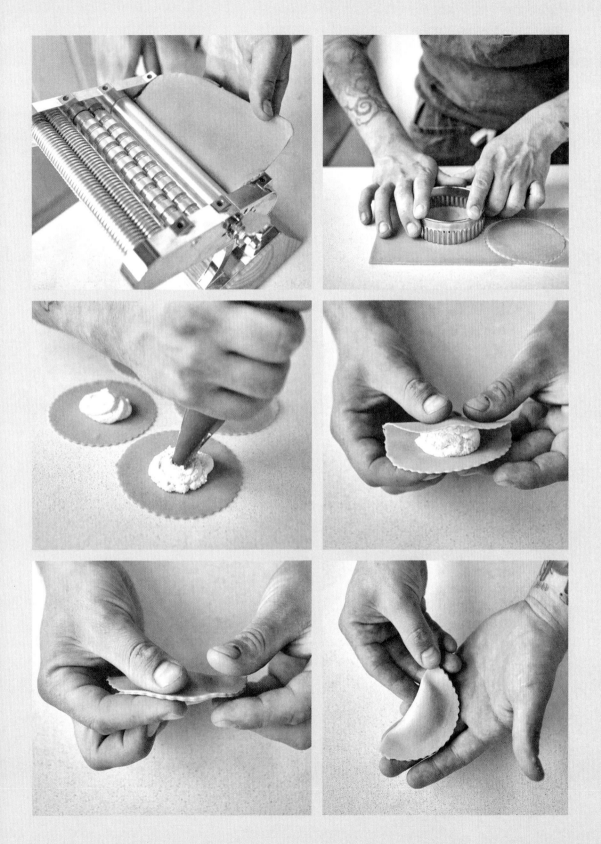

MEZZELUNE ALLA NORMA

Serves 4

400g/14oz herb-laminated egg dough (page 74)

For the filling

2 medium aubergines (eggplants), halved

30ml/2 tbsp olive oil

60g/2¼oz *pangrattato* (page 248)

grated zest of ½ lemon

10g/1/3oz Parmesan, grated

For the tomato sauce

75ml/5 tbsp olive oil, plus extra for drizzling

5 garlic cloves, thinly sliced

1 x 400g/14oz can of chopped tomatoes, or 500g/1lb 20z cherry tomatoes

To serve

handful of torn basil leaves

50g/2oz *ricotta salata*, pecorino or *pangrattato*

The Isle of Wight isn't that far from where I live, but it claims to have more sunshine than anywhere else in Britain – it's the Sicily of the English south coast. The Tomato Stall on the Isle of Wight is mad about all things tomato: they grow plum, beef, cherry, heritage varieties, and their boxes of tomatoes are famously colourful. I use them to make this sauce, along with some of their beautiful aubergines (eggplants), but you can always use a can of tomatoes if fresh tomatoes are not in season.

This shape looks extra special if you use laminated dough with fresh parsley or edible flowers. If you're careful when you cut them out, you can place the leaves to best effect in the centre of the half moon. Of course, you can use plain egg dough if you prefer – they will be just as tasty.

Preheat the oven to 190°C fan/410°F/gas mark 6. Score the flesh of the halved aubergines (eggplants) and place them on a baking sheet, drizzle with the olive oil and bake for 30 minutes. Remove from the oven and leave to one side until cool enough to handle.

Meanwhile, start on the tomato sauce. In a medium saucepan, heat 45ml/3 tablespoons of the olive oil. Add the garlic and fry on a low heat until fragrant, which will take about 1–2 minutes, then add the tomatoes and stir together. If using fresh tomatoes, once they have softened and split, mash them with the back of a spoon. Continue cooking for 20 minutes on a very low heat so the surface just bubbles from time to time. Now season with fine sea salt, add the remaining olive oil and leave on a gentle heat for a further 10–15 minutes. Leave to one side while you make the filling.

Using a tablespoon, scoop the aubergine flesh onto a chopping board and discard the skins. Roughly chop the aubergine flesh, gently squeezing to remove any excess moisture, and transfer to a clean bowl. Add the *pangrattato*, lemon zest and Parmesan, mix to combine, and season to taste with sea salt and freshly ground black pepper.

Continued overleaf

Vegan option

Use vegan semolina dough (page 41) instead of egg dough

Use nutritional yeast or *pangrattato* (page 248) instead of the cheese, to serve

Now you are ready to roll and fill the *mezzelune* (page 166).

When you've finished shaping the pasta, place the tomato sauce back on a medium-low heat.

Bring a large pan of water to the boil before adding a generous amount of table salt. Cook the *mezzelune* for 2–3 minutes, then, using a slotted spoon, transfer the pasta into the sauce. Gently swirl everything together, add most of the basil leaves and swirl one more time. Season to taste with sea salt and freshly ground black pepper, then sprinkle with the remaining basil.

Serve straightaway, finishing the dish with *ricotta salata* (if you have it) or the less traditional pecorino, or even *pangrattato* if you like. Not forgetting a glass of good red, of course.

MEZZELUNE FILLED WITH BEEF RAGÙ

Serves 4

400g/14oz classic egg dough (page 32)

90ml/6 tbsp olive oil

2 medium onions, diced

4 garlic cloves, finely chopped

2 carrots, diced

4 celery sticks, finely sliced

2 bay leaves

2 large sprigs of rosemary

sprig of sage

2 x 400g/14oz cans of plum tomatoes

500ml/generous 2 cups red wine

150ml/⅔ cup water

800g/1lb 12oz short rib beef, on the bone

60g/2¼oz Parmesan, finely grated

2 tsp dried oregano

On the way to visit the Molino Pasini flour mill, where my favourite 00 pasta flour is milled, I went for lunch with one of the owners, my friend Gianluca. We stopped in a small *osteria*, a quirky place with a glass-fronted fridge filled with sides of meat against one wall, and rough wooden tables which were set with folded linen napkins and wine glasses. We ate Parma ham melted over grilled polenta with chunks of Parmesan to start, followed by delicious slow-cooked beef *tortelloni*. This is my version of that very memorable dish.

Gently heat half the olive oil in a large ovenproof saucepan or casserole dish (preferably one with a lid). Add the onion, garlic, carrot and celery and cook the *soffritto* for 25 minutes on a medium heat. Tie all the herbs together with string, or place in a muslin (cheesecloth) spice bag if you have one, then add them to the *soffritto* along with the tomatoes, wine and water. Keep at a barely bubbling simmer while you sear the beef.

Preheat the oven to 220°C fan/475°F/gas mark 9. Season the meat by rubbing it all over with coarse sea salt and freshly ground black pepper. Transfer the beef to a heavy roasting tin and place in the oven for 15 minutes, turning the meat halfway to make sure it's browned all over. Remove from the oven and transfer the ribs to the casserole dish along with any juices in the tin. Cover with baking parchment and foil, or with a lid.

Reduce the oven temperature to 140°C fan/325°F/gas mark 3, then place the casserole in the oven and leave it to cook for 4–4½ hours, until the meat is tender and falling off the bone. Set to one side and allow to cool.

When the meat is cool enough to handle, lift it out and pick the meat off the bones (the bones can be discarded). Chop the meat finely, then place it in a colander set over a bowl along with the remaining vegetables and sauce from the casserole. The *ragù* needs to be a little on the dry side to use as a filling, so allow it to drain for 10 minutes.

Continued overleaf

FILLED PASTA & DUMPLINGS

Transfer the ragù to a large bowl, add the Parmesan and mix everything together well. Season to taste with sea salt and freshly ground black pepper, then place in the fridge for 20–30 minutes to allow the mixture to set a little.

Now you are ready to roll and fill the *mezzelune* (page 166).

When you've finished shaping the pasta, bring a large pan of water to the boil before adding table salt. Cook the *mezzelune* for 2–3 minutes.

While the pasta is cooking, add the remaining olive oil to a large saucepan along with half a ladleful of the pasta cooking water. Warm it over a medium heat, swirling the pan a little, then scatter over the oregano. Use a slotted spoon to transfer the pasta to the sauce and mix together to make sure the *mezzelune* are well coated in oil and herbs. Season to taste with sea salt and freshly ground black pepper before dividing between four warmed plates. Serve with a dressed green salad.

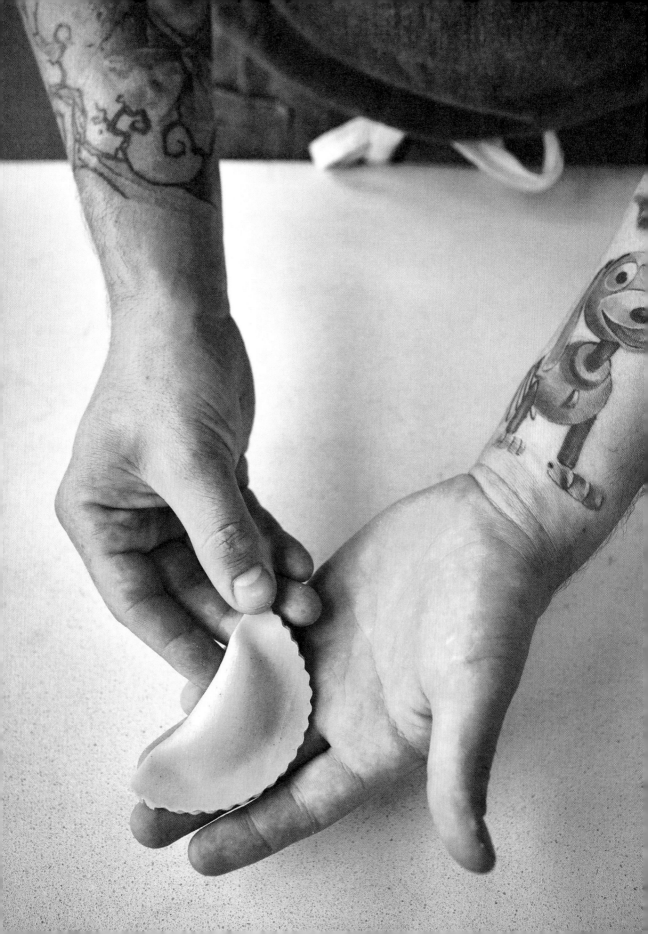

DOPPIO RAVIOLI

Equipment

pasta machine

ravioli cutter

2 piping bags (or 2 teaspoons)

small *garganelli* rolling pin
(if you have one)

pastry brush

If you're already a wizard at making *ravioli*, why not go a step further and make this double-filled version? It's a playful way of mixing and matching fillings, and the twin parcel is really easy to make. Try pairing herby mashed potato with *ragù*, or spiced pumpkin with creamy ricotta – there are lots of combinations to explore. I like to make this shape with rich egg dough (page 33).

Fill your piping bags with the pair of fillings you've made (see overleaf). If you don't have two piping bags, you can always use teaspoons, but a piping bag gives you a denser texture and more control over the exact placement of the filling.

Start with a quarter of the dough, keeping the rest in an airtight container, and prepare a tray or baking sheet dusted with coarse semolina, on which to lay out your finished pasta.

Roll out the dough to setting 7 on your pasta machine (page 60).

Lay the rolled sheet on a clean work surface and cut out rectangles roughly 11 x 7.5cm/4¼ x 3in. Pipe a line of filling across the short end of each rectangle, leaving a 1cm/½in gap at each edge, then do the same with the second filling at the opposite end.

Fold the dough over the first filling and then fold again to the centre, repeating this from the other end so that the two folds meet in the middle. Now use the *garganelli* pin, or the handle of a wooden spoon, to roll and pinch the sides together. If the dough is too dry to stick together, use a dab of water on a pastry brush to dampen the edges.

Use the *ravioli* cutter to trim the sides with the classic zig-zag edging, set on the prepared tray with and dust with a little extra semolina. Continue to roll and fill until all your double parcels are wrapped.

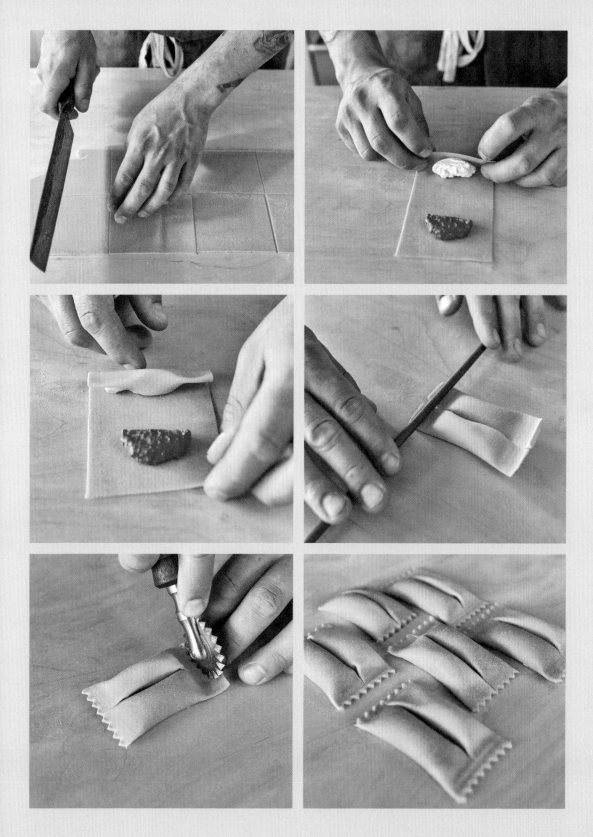

DOPPIO RAVIOLI FILLED WITH BEETROOT AND RICOTTA

Serves 4

400g/14oz rich egg dough (page 33)

For the beetroot (beets) filling

250g/9oz beetroot (beets), peeled and cut into small wedges

2 garlic cloves, peeled

2 tbsp olive oil

1 tbsp water

30g/1oz smoked almonds, plus extra to serve

30g/1oz Parmesan, grated, plus extra to serve

¼ tsp balsamic vinegar

For the ricotta filling

200g/7oz ricotta

grated zest of 1 lemon

30g/1oz Parmesan, grated

½ bunch of mint, leaves picked and chopped

For the butter sauce

75g/2¾oz butter

75ml/5 tbsp water

200g/7oz spinach leaves, washed and roughly chopped

This is a playful pasta – a double *ravioli* parcel that allows you to pair two fillings that complement one another. Here, I've paired earthy beetroot (beets) with herby ricotta, but you could try combos like potato and *ragù*, or white fish with peas and ricotta.

Preheat the oven to 180°C fan/400°F/gas mark 6. Line a roasting tin with a large sheet of foil add the beetroot (beets) and garlic, then drizzle over the olive oil and water. Fold the foil over so that it is closed at the top, like a loose parcel. Bake for 30 minutes, or until the beetroot is cooked (a knife should easily pierce the root). Leave to one side to cool a little.

Meanwhile, prepare the ricotta filling. In a large bowl, combine all the ingredients and season to taste with salt and pepper. Set to one side.

Place the beetroot, almonds, Parmesan and balsamic vinegar in the bowl of a food processor and blitz until everything is combined into a smooth-ish paste. Transfer to a small bowl and chill in the fridge for 30 minutes. If there's any oily beetroot juice in the base of the roasting tin, reserve it to spoon over the plated *ravioli*.

Now the fun starts: it's time to roll, fill and shape your *ravioli* (page 176).

Once all of your *ravioli* are made and ready to cook, make the butter sauce. Place the butter and water in a large saucepan over a medium heat. Shake the pan to combine the melting butter into the water to create a loose sauce; keep moving it around or you risk it splitting.

Meanwhile, set a large pan of water on the hob and, when the water is boiling, season it generously with table salt. Carefully drop in the *ravioli* and cook for 2–3 minutes.

When the pasta parcels are cooked, add them to the sauce, scatter over the chopped spinach and season to taste with sea salt and freshly ground black pepper. Continue to cook for a further 30 seconds or so until the spinach is wilted.

Divide between four warmed plates, with a grating of Parmesan or a scattering of flaked almonds over the top, and a drizzle of beetroot juice if you have any left over.

ANOLINI

Equipment

pasta machine

anolini stamp (mine is 3cm/1¼in) or a small round cookie cutter

piping bag (optional)

I'm a big fan of soups and broths, and in a Polish winter they are really good at warming you from the inside out. *Anolini*, traditionally filled with beef, pork and breadcrumbs, has the added advantage of bringing a hint of sunshine to your bowl, as the shapes are like small golden suns. The golden yellow colour of rich egg dough (page 33) make it ideal for this dish.

Start with a quarter of the dough, keeping the rest in an airtight container, and prepare a tray or baking sheet dusted with coarse semolina, on which to lay out your finished pasta.

Roll out the dough to setting 7 on your pasta machine (page 60).

Lay the rolled sheet on a clean work surface, fold it in half just to mark the middle of the length, then lay it flat again.

Place the filling in rows to one side of your marked line. Pipe or spoon a cherry-sized amount onto the dough, leaving a finger-width space on each side, and continue along the rows until you've filled all the space you can.

Carefully lift over the other half of the dough to cover, then just press between each mound to seal the outline of each shape. Now, using the *anolini* stamp, you can channel your inner Post Office counter clerk and start stamping – *bam, bam, bam!* And when you're really good, you can pick up speed and finish all the rows in seconds.

Gently lift away the off-cuts of pasta, which you can ball together and re-roll, or cut into smaller pieces to use as *maltagliati* (page 248).

Continue to roll and shape the rest of the dough until you have a trayful of beautiful sunshine.

TARRAGON AND MORTADELLA ANOLINI IN BRODO

Serves 4

400g/14oz rich egg dough
(page 33)

1 x quantity meat broth
(page 246)

250g/9oz *mortadella*

100g/3½oz ricotta

handful of tarragon, finely
chopped

grated zest and juice
of 1 lemon

Parmesan, to serve

Mortadella is often sold pre-sliced as it's a popular sandwich filling (if you haven't tried it in fresh, crusty focaccia, then put it on your to-do list). For this, you want to ask for a chunk of *mortadella* at the deli counter; if they have ends available, even better, as they are often sold at a discount and you'll be chopping the meat anyway. Don't splash out on the variety made with pistachio, just use the classic plain sausage; it will still carry plenty of flavour from the spices and the fat.

Start by making the broth, which ideally should be made a day ahead, depending on how long you like to simmer the bones. If you have more broth than you need for this dish you can easily freeze any leftovers.

For the pasta filling, start by roughly chopping the *mortadella* into small pieces, then place them into the bowl of a food processor and blitz until they break up. Add the ricotta, tarragon and lemon juice and zest, and blend until everything is well combined.

Scoop the *mortadella* filling into a bowl, season it with sea salt and freshly ground black pepper, and leave in the fridge for 30 minutes to firm up a little.

Roll, fill and shape the *anolini* (page 180) and re-heat your broth, making sure to check the seasoning once the broth is hot.

I prefer to cook the pasta separately in case any of them split (it's not great when this happens in your beautiful clear broth). Set a large pan of water on the hob and, when the water is boiling, season it generously with table salt. Carefully drop in the pasta and cook for 1½–2 minutes. Scoop out the pasta with a slotted spoon, or gently tip it into a colander to drain, then immediately divide it between four warmed bowls.

Ladle the hot broth over the *anolini* and finish with a generous grating of Parmesan.

RAVIOLO

Equipment

pasta machine

ravioli cutter or 10cm/4in cookie cutter

This pasta is something of a showstopper. Cut into the *raviolo* and the golden egg yolk spills across the plate, which always looks amazing, especially if you're using rich-yolk eggs.

This isn't pasta to serve a crowd, as you have to cook the *raviolo* in pairs at most, so that means you can't serve everyone at once, but the theatre of the food – and a glass of something cold – means that your dinner companions will happily wait their turn. The choice is yours, but I like to use rich egg dough (page 33) for this shape.

Start with a quarter of the dough, keeping the rest in an airtight container, and prepare a tray or baking sheet dusted with coarse semolina, on which to lay out your finished pasta.

Roll out the dough to setting 6 on your pasta machine (page 60).

Dust a clean work surface or board with semolina, place the sheet of pasta on top and then cut across it to create four pieces about 13cm/5in long.

Place a tablespoon of the filling into the centre of two of the rectangles and make a dip in the centre of each using the back of the spoon. Carefully drop the egg yolk into this dip; it should balance there like an egg in a nest.

Brush around the edge of the filling with the egg white to help seal the dough together, then place one of the plain sheets of pasta on top. Gently press around the filling, taking care not to split the egg yolk (this can be tricky the first time you try it but just work very slowly).

Trim the edges using a *raviolo* cutter, if you have one, otherwise use a sharp knife. Alternatively, you can create circular *raviolo* by using a large cookie cutter, preferably one with fluted edges to create a pretty parcel.

Gently set the finished parcels on the dusted tray and lightly dust with more semolina, then continue to roll and fill the remainder of the dough.

Keep any off-cuts of dough to use as *maltagliati* (page 248).

RAVIOLO WITH EGG YOLK AND RICOTTA

Serves 4 (makes 8)

400g/14oz rich egg dough (page 33)

30ml/2 tbsp olive oil

1 garlic clove, finely sliced

150g/5½oz spinach leaves, washed

2 Romano peppers, deseeded and roughly chopped

250g/9oz ricotta

50g/2oz sundried tomatoes, drained

20g/¾oz Parmesan, plus extra to serve

8 egg yolks (use 1 egg white to seal the *raviolo*)

80g/3oz butter, cubed

few sprigs of marjoram, leaves picked

Oddly, this pasta always makes me think of my favourite breakfast of soft-boiled eggs. There's nothing like cooking an egg to perfection and dipping into a golden yolk with a toasty buttered soldier. I admit this pasta dish is a bit more effort than boiling an egg, and you won't be able to serve everyone at once, but good things are always worth waiting for.

Heat 15ml/1 tablespoon of the olive oil in a large saucepan and fry the garlic for 30 seconds until fragrant before adding the spinach. Cook the spinach, turning it with a wooden spoon until it has wilted, then transfer to a sieve placed over a bowl to drain it of any excess moisture. Press the spinach with the back of the spoon so that it's as dry as possible, then place it in the bowl of a food processor.

Return the saucepan to a medium heat, add the remaining olive oil and fry the peppers until soft, which should take around 5 minutes. Add the peppers to the spinach, along with the ricotta, tomatoes and Parmesan. Blitz everything together for 30 seconds until you have a rough paste. Transfer to a clean bowl, season to taste with sea salt and freshly ground black pepper, and place in the fridge for at least 30 minutes to firm up a little.

Now for the fun part. Roll, fill and shape your *raviolo* (page 184).

Don't attempt to cook more than two or three *raviolo* at once as they are delicate, and you don't want to split the egg yolks. It's best to play it safe to begin with and cook two together.

Bring a large pan of water to the boil before adding a generous amount of table salt. At the same time, place the butter into a large saucepan with half a ladleful of boiling water and swish it around to melt and emulsify the butter. Add a twist or two of freshly ground black pepper and keep warm on the lowest heat you can.

Cook the *raviolo* for 90 seconds, taking good care not to split the parcels. Carefully lift them out of the pan using a slotted spoon and place them in the butter sauce. Turn the heat to medium, scatter over the marjoram leaves and gently swish around in the butter. Now you are ready to serve these, as you continue to cook the remaining pasta.

ROTOLO

Equipment

pasta machine

rolling pin

ruler

palette knife or spatula

muslin cloth (cheesecloth)
or light tea (dish) towel

string

I first came across this rather unusual shape at a pasta event in London. I was most impressed with the *rotolo* made by my friend Big Has: a pasta roulade rolled, boiled, sliced and then served in a brown butter sauce. Wow. For this shape you need to roll the dough in one piece – you could cut the dough into two and roll them separately, but I find you get a more consistent result if you roll in one then cut the sheet afterwards. I use classic egg dough (page 32) here.

Following the method on page 60, roll out your pasta dough, stopping at setting 6. A full rolled sheet of dough will be about 130cm/50in long, so fold it over itself as you roll it – three folds will give you four equal pieces. Just make sure to dust it with 00 flour if it's sticky.

Now unfold the dough and cut across the fold lines to make four pieces – or just use a ruler. Turn the rectangles so that the short ends are facing you, overlap each piece by about 1cm/½in, then use the rolling pin to connect the four pieces back together; your dough should be moist enough for them to stick to one another easily with the pressure of your rolling pin. The final size should be around 30x50cm/12x20in.

Using a palette knife or spatula, spread the filling across the pasta sheet, leaving a clear 2.5cm/1in around the edges. Now create your roll, starting at the short end. Using both hands, gently lift the dough, fold it over the filling, then roll to the end. Don't roll too tightly or you'll squeeze the filling out, but keep a nice firm shape, as if you were making a Swiss roll. When you get to the end, simply brush the clear dough with water, then pinch the ends together to seal.

Lay your muslin or tea (dish) towel on the work surface and lift the *rotolo* onto the bottom edge of the cloth. Roll the cloth up from the bottom, rolling both the cloth and the pasta away from you until the *rotolo* is covered, then tie the ends of the cloth together with string. It's best to tie a couple of pieces of string around the middle as well – you don't want the whole thing to fall apart as it's boiled, which you're now ready to do. (This is explained overleaf in the following recipe.)

FILLED PASTA & DUMPLINGS

BAKED ROTOLO WITH RICOTTA, BROAD BEANS AND PETIT POIS

Serves 4–6

200g/7oz classic egg dough (page 32) (I suggest you make the full quantity of 400g/14oz, use half and freeze the remainder)

For the filling

240g/8½oz frozen broad (fava) beans

140g/5½oz frozen petit pois

400g/14oz ricotta

grated zest of 2 lemons

80g/3oz Parmesan

For the tomato sauce

60ml/4 tbsp olive oil

5 garlic cloves, finely chopped

2 x 400g/14oz cans of plum tomatoes or 600g/1lb 5oz cherry tomatoes

To finish

olive oil, to drizzle

grated Parmesan, to serve

basil and mint leaves, to serve

I'd suggest saving this pasta for a special occasion, or at least the weekend – it's not one to throw together after a hard day at work – but it's fun to make and an unusual dish to serve instead of the more familiar *lasagne* or *cannelloni*.

First make the tomato sauce. Pour the olive oil into a large saucepan on a medium heat, fry the garlic for a couple of minutes until fragrant but without letting it colour. Add the tomatoes (leave the cherry tomatoes whole, if using) and cook for 40 minutes on a medium-low heat, stirring occasionally. Half-cover the pan with a lid so that the tomatoes don't spit and splash as they bubble away.

At the end of the cooking time, break up any tomatoes with the back of a wooden spoon if they haven't already split. Season to taste with sea salt and freshly ground black pepper and leave to one side.

Now make the *rotolo* filling. Blanch the frozen broad (fava) beans by placing them in a large heatproof bowl and covering them with boiling water. Leave them for 2 minutes, then drain and peel them. The skins should come away easily and can be discarded.

Defrost the frozen peas by the same method: pour boiling water over them and leave for 1 minute. Drain the water, then place both the peas and the beans into the bowl of a food processor along with the rest of the filling ingredients. Blend them together to create a rough creamy paste flecked with green.

Make and fill the *rotolo* following the instructions on page 188.

When your *rotolo* is wrapped and ready to cook, bring a large pan of water to the boil (check that the wrapped pasta will fit in the pan; you can gently curl it round a little if you need to). Season the boiling water with a generous amount of table salt, then carefully lift the *rotolo* into the pan.

Cook for 18 minutes at a steady rolling boil. Bear in mind that you can't check that the pasta is cooked through – which is why I suggest you use a timer set for 18 minutes – it's better for the pasta to be softer rather than to have any part undercooked.

FILLED PASTA & DUMPLINGS

Preheat the oven to 180°C fan/400°F/gas mark 6. Prepare a baking dish or casserole dish by spreading the tomato sauce across the base.

Carefully drain the water and lift the *rotolo* onto a clean board. Cut the string and unwrap the cloth, slice the *rotolo* into eight equal pieces and tuck them cut-side-up in the sauce. Drizzle with olive oil and bake for 15 minutes until the edges of the pasta start to turn crispy and golden brown. Remove from the oven and scatter over the Parmesan and herbs.

Place on the table with a flourish – you deserve a round of applause here – along with a bowl of green salad or a pan of garlicky buttered spinach.

CARAMELLE

Equipment

pasta machine

piping bag (optional)

Caramelle are like little Christmas crackers, prompting the question – what's inside them? Usually pumpkin with Gorgonzola dolce when I'm in charge. People love food that's shaped like sweets (candy), and serving *caramelle* usually brings a smile to the faces around the dinner table.

Being playful with the dough colours is a bit like creating your own sweet (candy) wrappers too (see page 200) – if you're patient and sketch out your idea on paper first, you can define exactly where the stripes will fall on each piece. Challenge accepted!

You can use vegan semolina dough (page 41) for this shape, but I prefer to use egg doughs as they're a bit more delicate and give a finer result.

Start with a quarter of the dough, keeping the rest in an airtight container, and prepare a tray or baking sheet dusted with coarse semolina, on which to lay out your finished pasta.

Roll out the dough to setting 7 on your pasta machine (page 60).

Lay the rolled sheet flat on the work surface or a board and cut out rectangles to a size of around 7x9cm/2¾x3½in.

Place about a heaped teaspoon of filling at the bottom centre of the longer side of each rectangle. Using a piping bag gives you more precision and a slightly denser filling (because it's compressed as it's pushed through the nozzle), but you can use a teaspoon if you prefer. Fold the dough over twice to create a small tube, press your index fingers into the dough at either end of the filling to seal it inside, then pleat the outer long edges together to create a shape like a small wrapped sweet (candy). Now use your fingertip to make a dip in the centre of each *caramelle*, creating a little crater to catch the sauce.

Place each *caramelle* onto the prepared tray, then continue to roll, shape and fill the remainder of the dough.

CARAMELLE WITH SWEET POTATO AND GOATS' CHEESE

Serves 4

400g/14oz rich egg dough
(page 33)

For the sweet potato filling

500g/1lb 2oz sweet potato
(1 large or 2 small), scrubbed

125g/4½oz goats' cheese

20g/¾oz Parmesan,
finely grated

grated zest and juice of
½ lemon

small bunch of parsley, leaves
picked and chopped

For the cheese sauce

60g/2¼oz butter, cubed

300g/10½oz spinach leaves,
washed and roughly chopped

To serve

30g/1oz almond flakes
or pine nuts

pecorino or Parmesan, grated

Whenever Richard our plumber is nearby, he drops in for a cup of Yorkshire tea and a chat – and cake if there is any on the go (which more often than not there is). It turns out that he used to work as a cheese-maker at a Somerset goat dairy and that, back in the day, they would fill 5cm/2in cut drainpipes with the goats' curd and leave it to set overnight. Perhaps being surrounded by drainpipes inspired his change of career...

Here, I use a firm goats' cheese for the *caramelle* filling, rather than a soft cheese with a rind; you want something crumbly rather than creamy.

Preheat the oven to 190°C fan/410°F/gas mark 6. Halve the sweet potato if you're using a large one, otherwise leave them whole. Prick all over with a fork and bake until fully cooked, which should take around 35 minutes. Leave to one side to cool down.

While the oven is on, toast the almond flakes or pine nuts. Scatter them on a baking sheet and place it on the lower shelf of the oven for 5–6 minutes until they look golden brown (keep a close eye on them as nuts have a horrible tendency to burn when you don't pay attention to them). Set to one side.

When the potatoes are cool enough to handle, scoop out the flesh and discard the skins. Use a potato ricer if you have one, otherwise mash the potato in a medium bowl; you should end up with around 310g/11oz mashed potato. Combine with the rest of the filling ingredients and season with sea salt and freshly ground black pepper.

Roll, fill and shape the *caramelle* (page 192).

Place the butter in a saucepan, add a ladleful of warm water and set it over a low heat. As the butter starts to melt, swirl it around the pan to combine with the water, then add the spinach, cover with a lid and cook for 2 minutes until the spinach has wilted. Season to taste.

Continued overleaf

FILLED PASTA & DUMPLINGS

Vegan option

Replace the egg dough with vegan semolina dough (page 41)

Use 60g/2¼oz *pangrattato* (page 248) instead of the goats' cheese

Replace the pecorino and Parmesan with the same amount of nutritional yeast

Make the sauce with olive oil instead of butter

Meanwhile, cook the pasta. Set a large pan of water on the hob and, when the water is boiling, season it generously with table salt. Drop the pasta into the boiling water and cook for 2–3 minutes. Carefully drain the pasta, taking care not to split any of the parcels.

While the pasta is cooking, arrange the spinach on four warmed plates, then divide the *caramelle* between them. Scatter the toasted nuts over the top and finish with a grating of pecorino or Parmesan.

CARAMELLE WITH DUCK AND PICKLED RHUBARB

400g/14oz rich egg dough (page 33)

For the filling

60ml/4 tbsp olive oil

1 onion, finely chopped

1 carrot, finely chopped

1 celery stick, finely chopped

1 garlic clove, finely chopped

1 star anise

½ cinnamon stick

4 cloves

200ml/generous ¾ cup white wine

3 duck legs

40g/1½oz Parmesan, finely grated

For the butter sauce

100g/3½oz butter, diced

grated zest of 1 orange

For the pickled rhubarb

2 sticks of pink rhubarb, thinly sliced

200g/7oz vinegar

200g/7oz sugar

20ml/4 tsp water

To serve

dill or fennel tops

Parmesan

I once worked alongside Dr Johnny Drain (known as the Walter White of flavour) who, among his many diverse food interests, is obsessed with pickles and ferments. One January he pickled some early Yorkshire rhubarb – always surprisingly pink and a welcome sight in grey midwinter. When I tried it, I knew straightaway that I wanted to serve it with a duck-filled pasta. Sometimes these crazy ideas just work. I've used rich egg dough (page 33) here, but this also works well with stripy dough (pages 68–70) made using 200g/7oz cocoa egg dough (page 54) and 200g/7oz rich egg dough.

For the filling, heat half the olive oil in a medium pan (one that has a lid) on a medium heat, then add the onion, carrot, celery and garlic and cook for 5 minutes, stirring occasionally. Place the star anise, cinnamon stick and cloves in a small muslin cloth (cheesecloth), or a spice bag if you have one, add it to the *soffritto* and continue cooking for a further 15 minutes, stirring occasionally. Reduce the heat to low, add the white wine and cook for another 5 minutes.

Meanwhile, season the duck legs with sea salt and freshly ground black pepper. Add the other half of the olive oil to a frying pan (skillet), place on a medium heat, add the duck legs and sear on both sides until they are nice and bronzed. This should take around 3 minutes on each side. Transfer to the pan of *soffritto*, adding enough water to cover the duck legs. Cover with a lid and cook on a medium-low heat for 2 hours, giving the pan an occasional shake to make sure nothing sticks to the bottom.

When the duck is cooked, the meat should pull easily from the bones. Take the pan off the heat, discard the spices and allow everything to cool down.

When the duck is cool enough to handle, pick the meat off the bones (discarding the bones), roughly chop the meat and transfer it to a clean bowl. Drain the remaining vegetables from the pan and add them to the bowl along with the Parmesan. Mix everything together and leave to one side to firm up a little.

Continued overleaf

Next make a quick pickle. If you have a mandoline, use it to slice the rhubarb as you'll get lovely fine strips, otherwise you can use a vegetable peeler. Place the prepared rhubarb into a heatproof container or bowl and set aside. Add the vinegar, sugar and water to a small saucepan and bring to the boil. Take off the heat as soon as the sugar dissolves and carefully pour the liquor over the rhubarb. Cover with a plate or baking parchment and leave to one side for 20 minutes. Remember that you can re-use the pickling liquor a couple of times (try finely sliced carrots, fennel or onion, all good in salads or in a cheese toastie).

Roll, shape and fill the *caramelle* (page 192).

Set a large pan of water on the hob and, when the water is boiling, season it generously with table salt. At the same time, place a large saucepan on a medium heat with the butter, orange zest and a ladleful of water. Drop the pasta into the boiling water and cook for 2–3 minutes, then use a slotted spoon to transfer the pasta into the saucepan. Cook the butter sauce by gently moving the pasta around with a wooden spoon. Season to taste.

Share between four warmed plates, scatter the dill or fennel on top and place soft strips of pickled rhubarb around the pasta.

Serve with some more Parmesan if you fancy, along with a dressed fresh green salad.

SFOGLIA LORDA

Equipment

pasta machine or *mattarello* (pasta rolling pin)

spatula

ravioli cutter

These little squares enclose a barely-there cheese filling and were originally made using any leftover filling from making *cappelletti*. Frugal Emilia-Romagna housewives would spread the mixture of fresh and aged cheese onto sheets of dough traditionally rolled by hand – *sfoglia* – then folded together and cut into squares with a *ravioli* cutter.

You can use a pasta machine to roll out the dough, as it's much easier to create the thin pasta sheet you need, but if you'd like to, this is a good shape with which to practise your hand-rolling skills and channel an Italian *nonna*. I like to use classic (page 32) or rich egg dough (page 33) for this shape.

Start with a quarter of the dough, keeping the rest in an airtight container, and prepare a tray or baking sheet dusted with coarse semolina, on which to lay out your finished pasta.

Roll out the dough to setting 7 on your pasta machine (page 60).

If you're rolling by hand, use a *mattarello* if you have one: aim for a sheet so thin that it is almost transparent. You should be able to see your fingers through it when you lift it (Italian housewives were said to hold it up to the window to see if they could see the church tower through it – try it if you have such a view from your window!).

Lay the rolled sheet of dough on the work surface and fold it in half to mark the middle, then unfold it again so that it's flat. On one side of the mark, use a spatula to spread a thin layer of the filling, then fold the dough back over to sandwich the filling. Press gently to remove any air pockets and prick all over with a fork (this is to stop them splitting when they are cooked).

Using the *ravioli* cutter, cut the filled dough into 2x2cm/¾x¾in squares. The cutter helps to seal the edges as you go, so there's less chance of the filling leaking out. Any off-cuts can simply be cut into rough shapes and used in the same dish (it can't be re-rolled as it contains the cheese filling).

Place your finished shapes on the dusted tray and continue rolling and filling until you've used up all the dough.

SFOGLIA LORDA
IN BRODO

Serves 4

For the broth

1 x quantity meat broth (made with chicken) (page 246)

OR

1 x quantity Parmesan broth (page 108)

OR

1 x quantity butter tomato sauce (page 120)

For the dough

400g/14oz classic egg dough (page 32)

250g/9oz ricotta

80g/3oz Parmesan, grated, plus extra to serve

1 egg

grated zest of 1 lemon

½ nutmeg

The beauty of this shape is that it can be used in a light broth or a thicker soup, or it can be served with a tomato sauce, butter sage sauce or even pesto. It's a pasta that kids like to make as well as eat, so why not get them involved, even if it's just to roll the *ravioli* cutter over the dough to make the squares.

You will need to cook the chicken broth well in advance of making the pasta, as you need to roast the bones and simmer the broth for a few hours. However, the Parmesan broth can be made alongside the pasta, as you can just keep an eye on it while it's simmering on the hob.

First, make your chosen broth or sauce. The meat broth will need to be prepped in advance, but if you're making the Parmesan broth or the tomato sauce, then you can prepare these as you make and shape the pasta.

For the pasta filling, place the ricotta in a muslin cloth (cheesecloth) and squeeze out the excess liquid (you will lose around 15 per cent of the weight). Transfer to a large bowl and add the Parmesan, egg and lemon zest and mix together using a wooden spoon. Grate a generous amount of nutmeg over and mix again, then set aside in the fridge for 30 minutes.

When you're ready to use the filling, season with sea salt and freshly ground black pepper.

Roll, shape and fill the *sfoglia lorda* (page 202).

When you are ready to serve, carefully drop the pasta into the hot broth or sauce. Bring to a boil and let the pasta cook for 2 minutes.

I like to carry the pan to the dinner table and serve with an extra chunk of Parmesan to let everyone grate their own cheese.

SCARPINOCC

Equipment

pasta machine

kitchen knife

piping bag (optional)

A shape reminiscent of *caramelle*, and very similar to make, the name originates from the word *scarpa*, a shoe shaped in the style of an old-fashioned wooden clog (very familiar to me from my Polish dentist, who wears them all the time).

In Lombardy, where this shape comes from, the filling would traditionally be made with semi-soft Taleggio cheese and breadcrumbs (Taleggio is delicious melted over minted new potatoes in spring, or better still, in a cheese toastie). Sauces tend to be simple, and the little dip in the centre of the *scarpinocc* is perfect for catching the buttery balsamic sauce. You can use any dough, but I like to use classic (page 32) or rich egg dough (page 33) for this shape.

Start with a quarter of the dough, keeping the rest in an airtight container, and prepare a tray or baking sheet dusted with coarse semolina, on which to lay out your finished pasta.

Roll out the dough to setting 7 on your pasta machine (page 60).

Lay the dough flat on a work surface or board and cut out squares to a size of around 7x7cm/2¾x2¾in.

Pipe the filling along the centre of each square and wrap the dough over to make a tube shape. Now pinch each end of the dough between two fingers at the same time as pressing down slightly and you will have sealed the ends with the distinctive inverted T shape. All you need to do now is create the satisfying dimple by pressing the plump centre with your index finger. *Boom!*

Place each *scarpinocc* onto your tray to make sure they don't stick, then continue to roll, fill and shape the remainder of the dough.

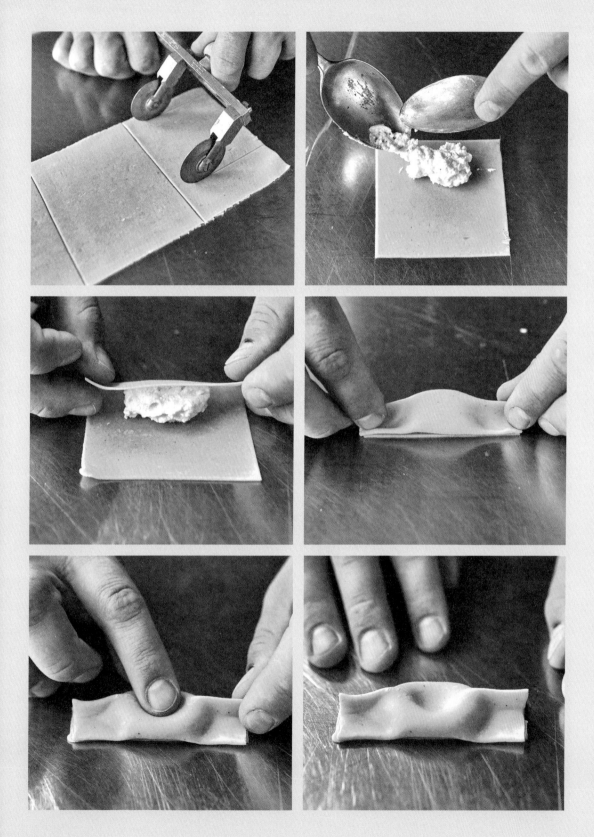

SCARPINOCC WITH CRAB AND SPICY 'NDUJA

Serves 4

400g/14oz rich egg dough
(page 33)

For the filling

250g/9oz white crab meat

grated zest of 2 lemons

80g/3oz 'nduja

½ bunch of parsley, finely
chopped

80g/3oz mascarpone

20g/¾oz breadcrumbs

For the sauce

500ml/2 cups oat milk

200g/7oz ground almonds

grated zest of 1 lemon

1 garlic clove, crushed

5g/1 tsp nutritional yeast
or Parmesan

30ml/2 tbsp olive oil

To serve

handful of agretti or samphire
(or rainbow chard)

green oil (optional)
(page 249)

Sometimes on a summer weekend afternoon at West Bay, Dorset, we will see groups of kids around the quayside with their crab-catching kit: bacon, string, and a bucket of seawater to keep their catch in. It looks like good fun, but probably not the best way to bag your supper, so I head to the fishmonger for crab instead.

Start by picking over the crab meat with your fingers to make sure all tiny pieces of shell are removed. Transfer to a medium bowl together with the rest of the filling ingredients and mix with a wooden spoon to combine. As the 'nduja is spicy and there's plenty of lemon juice, you shouldn't need to season the filling, but check it's to your taste. Leave in the fridge until ready to use.

Place the oat milk, almonds, lemon zest, garlic and nutritional yeast or Parmesan in a saucepan and cook on a medium heat for 35–40 minutes, stirring occasionally. You might need to add a touch more oat milk or water if the sauce looks a bit too thick. Transfer the mixture to a blender (or use a stick blender) and blitz everything together, adding the olive oil slowly at the same time. Don't be tempted to pour all the olive oil in at once or the sauce may split. Transfer to a clean saucepan and set to one side.

Now make and fill the scarpinocc (page 206). When they are ready to cook, set a large pan of water on the hob and, once the water is boiling, season it generously with table salt. At the same time, warm the sauce through by setting it on a low heat, and blanch the agretti or samphire by dropping it into a small pan of boiling water for 1–2 minutes (if you can't find either of these, use chopped chard leaves instead).

Cook the pasta for 2 minutes. While it's cooking, share the sauce between four warmed shallow bowls.

Drain the pasta – you don't need to reserve any of the pasta cooking water for this dish – and place the scarpinocc on top of the sauce. Scatter over the agretti or samphire along with a drizzle of green oil, if you like.

TORTELLI CON LA CODA

Equipment

pasta machine

kitchen knife or *bicicletta*

Con la coda means 'with a tail', and these shapes do look a lot like little fish; as well as having a tail, the plaited tops look like scales. This shape is not very common – like many of the more difficult shapes to master, they tend to stay as local specialities in their region. Sometimes called *tortellini Piacentini*, *tortelli con la coda* originates from the small town of Piacenza in Emilia-Romagna, and is traditionally filled with ricotta, spinach and nutmeg. You can use any dough, but I like to use classic (page 32) or rich egg dough (page 33) for this shape.

Start with a quarter of the dough, keeping the rest in an airtight container, and prepare a tray or baking sheet dusted with coarse semolina, on which to lay out your finished pasta.

Roll out the dough to setting 7 on your pasta machine (page 60).

Lay the rolled sheet on a clean work surface and, using a sharp kitchen knife (or a *bicicletta* if you have one), cut the sheet into squares, roughly 7.5x7.5cm/3x3in. Place a teaspoon of filling in the centre of each square. Place a square flat in the palm of one hand, then, starting at one corner, fold and tuck one side and then the other over the filling, ending with a little twist to create the characteristic fish-tail shape. You may squeeze out some of the filling as you go, but just pinch it off as needed to seal the end firmly.

Place each *tortelli* on the prepared tray and carry on shaping the rest of the dough.

SALMON TORTELLI
CON LA CODA WITH
BUTTER SAUCE

Serves 4

200g/7oz rich egg dough
(page 33)

200g/7oz spinach or spirulina
dough (pages 48, 54 or 56)

For the filling

2 salmon fillets (around
380g/13oz)

45ml/3 tbsp olive oil

80g/3oz mascarpone

50g/2oz panko breadcrumbs,
toasted

grated zest and juice
of 1 lemon

1½ tbsp capers, chopped

bunch of parsley, leaves
picked and chopped

For the sauce

100g/3½oz butter, cubed

½ bunch of agretti,
leaves picked

juice of ½ lemon (optional)

Agretti, sometimes sold as monk's beard, isn't always easy to get hold of – you're unlikely to find it in any supermarket – but we're really lucky to be able to source it from Lally and Tomas at our local Saturday market in Dorset. The dark green fleshy leaves are fresh-flavoured and hint of the sea (agretti is similar to samphire), and are delicious served drizzled with lemon juice and olive oil. It's a perfect pairing with a fillet of fish or a *burrata*. Here, I use it to finish a bowl of salmon *tortelli*, adding lemony crunch to complement the soft pasta. If you can't find agretti you can use samphire, or just garnish the dish with plenty of chopped dill instead.

Season the salmon by scattering sea salt on both sides of the fillets. Warm the olive oil in a heavy-based frying pan (skillet) on a medium-high heat. When you see the texture of the oil change – it will appear thinner when it's hot – add the fish and reduce the heat to medium. Fry for 4–5 minutes on each side until just cooked; the fillets should still be soft and moist. Set aside to rest and cool a little.

When they are cool enough to handle, use your fingers to flake the salmon fillets into a medium bowl. Combine with the remaining filling ingredients and season to taste with sea salt and freshly ground black pepper. Place in the fridge for at least half an hour to firm up a little; the breadcrumbs will absorb some of the moisture to create a firmer filling.

Now you are ready to make and fill the *tortelli* (page 210).

Bring a large pan of water to the boil before adding some table salt. Now is a good time to blanch the agretti: just drop it into the water and cook for a minute before lifting out using a slotted spoon or tongs. Set aside. Then add the *tortelli* to the pan and cook them for 2–3 minutes.

Meanwhile, place the butter and a ladleful of pasta cooking water into a large saucepan set over a medium heat. Stir occasionally, then add the cooked pasta and blanched agretti. Swirl everything together until the sauce thickens a little. Season with sea salt, freshly ground black pepper and lemon juice, if desired, then divide between four warmed plates. *Buon appetito!*

SACCHETTI

Equipment

pasta machine

ravioli cutter or kitchen knife

piping bag (optional)

There are two ways to shape *sacchetti* ('little bags'), depending on which style of bag you prefer. I like the square rather than the round shape as I think it cooks more evenly and it's easier to plate nicely, so this is the shape I'm sharing here. I like to use classic egg dough (page 32) to make this shape.

Start with a quarter of the dough, keeping the rest in an airtight container, and prepare a tray or baking sheet dusted with coarse semolina, on which to lay out your finished pasta.

Roll out the dough to setting 7 on your pasta machine (page 60).

Lay the rolled dough flat on the work surface and use a *ravioli* cutter or kitchen knife to cut out squares to a size of around 7x7cm/ 2¾x2¾in.

Pipe or spoon the filling into the centre of each square. Pull two sides up to cover the filling and then press the side edges together, leaving the top open. Now push the top corners together over the filling to connect them in the middle, creating a classic pyramid shape. Seal the remaining two sides. Your pyramid – or little square bag – is complete. Place on the prepared tray and carry on shaping the rest of the dough.

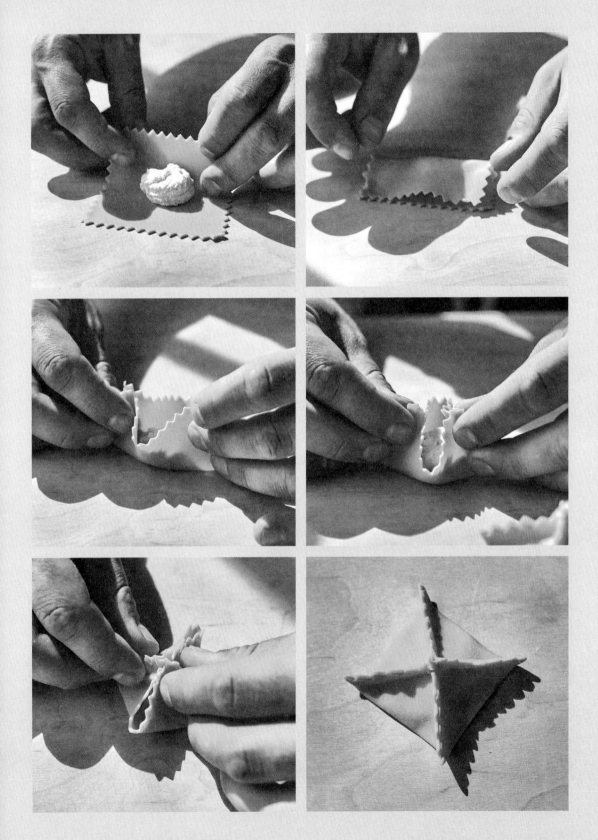

SACCHETTI WITH RICOTTA, ASPARAGUS, COURGETTES AND PEAS

Serves 4

400g/14oz classic egg dough
(page 32)

1 courgette (zucchini), around
150g/5½oz

100g/3½oz asparagus, trimmed

40g/1½oz frozen peas

grated zest of 1 lemon

250g/9oz ricotta

80g/3oz butter, cubed

Parmesan or pecorino,
to serve

My friend Steve's asparagus patch is his pride and joy, and rightly so. Sometimes on a late spring weekend he comes round to ask what time we'll be eating supper. When he first asked this I was puzzled, thinking that he was maybe hoping to join us, but then he explained that fresh asparagus ideally needs to be eaten within 30 minutes of picking, so he wanted to time the delivery accordingly. Occasionally he brings so much asparagus that we simply eat it with butter and sea salt and still have enough left to make this filled pasta as well.

Coarsely grate the courgette (zucchini) and place it in a sieve resting over a bowl. Sprinkle with a pinch of table salt and roughly mix, then leave for 10 minutes to allow the courgette to drain excess moisture.

In a medium saucepan, blanch the asparagus for 90 seconds in plenty of boiling water. Lift it out using a slotted spoon or tongs and set aside to cool. Use the same water to defrost the peas for 30 seconds, then drain them and add to the bowl of a food processor.

Chop the asparagus spears in half, squeeze any moisture from the courgette and add them both to the food processor, together with the lemon zest and ricotta. Pulse until you have a creamy flecked green mixture. Transfer to a clean bowl, season to taste with sea salt and freshly ground black pepper, then leave in the fridge until you are ready to fill the *sacchetti*.

Now it's time to roll, fill and shape your pasta (page 214).

Place a small saucepan on a medium heat and add the butter. Swirl the pan from time to time to make sure the butter is cooking evenly. Cook until the butter browns and you smell its lovely, nutty flavour, then take off the heat and strain into a large saucepan (this is to avoid any dark brown bits spoiling the texture of the sauce).

Bring a large pan of water to the boil before adding a generous amount of table salt, and cook the *sacchetti* for 2 minutes. Add a small ladleful of the pasta cooking water to the brown butter and put it back on a medium heat. Using a slotted spoon or spider strainer, carefully transfer the pasta to the sauce and gently combine. Serve straightaway, with a scattering of Parmesan or pecorino on top.

CASONCELLI

Equipment

pasta machine or *mattarello* (pasta rolling pin)

kitchen knife

This pasta looks like a wrapped boiled sweet (candy), and they are actually sometimes made with a sweet filling; raisins or crushed amaretti biscuits serve as a counterpoint to the fat of pork or beef. Not one I've tried yet, but I will if I ever visit Bergamo.

Typical of the Lombardy region in northern Italy, *casoncelli* are usually filled with meat, breadcrumbs and cheese, and often served tossed in *burro e salvia* – butter sage sauce – a musky aromatic herb that I'm lucky enough to have in the garden. You can use any dough, but I like to use classic (page 32) or rich egg dough (page 33) for this shape.

Start with a quarter of the dough, keeping the rest in an airtight container, and prepare a tray or baking sheet dusted with coarse semolina, on which to lay out your finished pasta.

Roll out the dough to setting 7 on your pasta machine (page 60), or use a rolling pin if you prefer (or if you're practising your hand rolling technique).

Lay the rolled dough flat on the work surface and, using a kitchen knife, cut out squares roughly 7.5x7.5cm/3x3in. Place a teaspoon of the filling in one corner of each square. Lift that corner and fold the dough over the filling twice. Press firmly on either side of the mound with your fingertips to seal.

Place the *casoncelli* on the prepared tray and carry on shaping the rest of the dough.

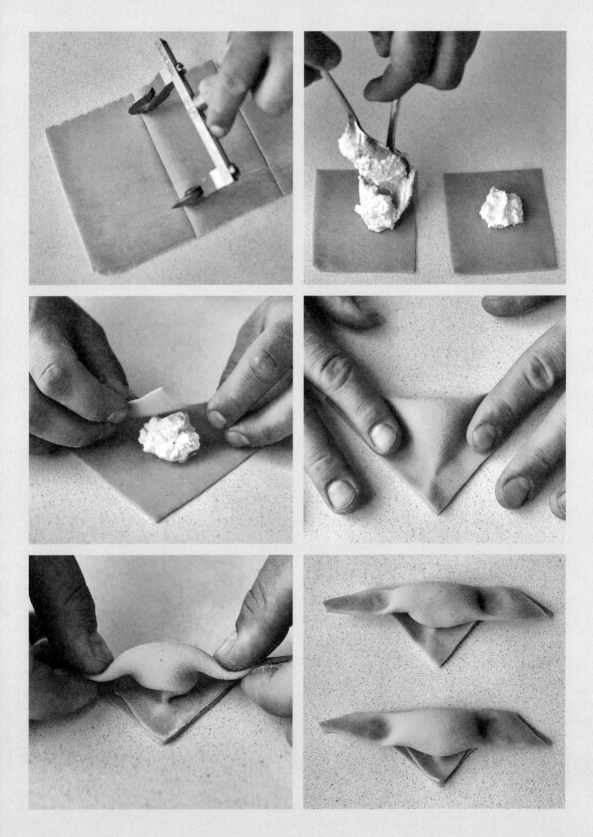

CASONCELLI WITH MUSHROOMS AND TALEGGIO

Serves 4

400g/14oz classic egg dough (page 32)

For the filling

30ml/2 tbsp olive oil

1 small onion, diced

2 garlic cloves, finely chopped

240g/8½oz oyster mushrooms, finely chopped

½ tsp table salt

100g/3½oz Taleggio cheese, rind removed

30g/1oz *pangrattato* (page 248), plus extra to serve

For the brown butter sauce

80g/3oz butter, cubed

handful of sage leaves

pecorino, to serve

Taleggio is a mild-flavoured, washed-rind cheese named after the Alpine valley where it was first made. Its creamy texture makes it a great melting cheese. Here it works perfectly with oyster mushrooms and *pangrattato* to make the filling for *casoncelli*.

Heat the olive oil in a medium saucepan, add the onion and garlic and cook for 5–7 minutes on a medium heat until they start to turn golden. Stir occasionally to ensure the garlic doesn't catch.

Add the chopped mushrooms and cook for 2 minutes, then add the salt and continue cooking for 10 minutes, stirring occasionally. If you are using chestnut mushrooms, make sure you cook until all of their liquid has gone (they contain more moisture than oyster mushrooms). When the mushrooms are cooked, leave the pan to one side.

Roughly chop the Taleggio and place it in a large bowl with the *pangrattato*, then add the mushroom mixture and stir well. This will give you a rough-textured filling; if you'd prefer a smooth filling, pulse in a food processor instead. Place in the fridge for 20 minutes.

Now you are ready to make and fill the *casoncelli* (page 218).

Once the pasta is ready to cook, make the brown butter sauce. Place a small saucepan on a medium heat and add the butter. Swirl to make sure the butter melts evenly, then cook until the butter browns and you smell its lovely, nutty flavour. Take off the heat and strain into a large saucepan (this is to avoid any dark brown bits spoiling the texture of the sauce).

In the meantime, cook the *casoncelli*. Bring a large pan of water to the boil before adding salt. Cook the pasta for 2–3 minutes.

Add a small ladleful of the pasta cooking water to the brown butter and put it back on a medium heat. Using a slotted spoon or spider strainer, carefully transfer the pasta to the sauce and gently swirl to combine. Add the sage leaves and swirl one more time, then season to taste with salt and pepper.

Divide between four warmed plates and serve with steamed broccoli, along with some *pangrattato* or pecorino (I'm having both).

AGNOLINI MANTOVANI

Equipment

pasta machine

ravioli cutter

piping bag (if you like)

Panificio Freddi is a family-run bakery and pasta shop in Mantova, northern Italy, run by Rossana and her son Riccardo. In 2023 they celebrated the centenary of their extraordinary business, initially making and selling pasta from their shop and now distributing it right across Emilia-Romagna. Walking into the handsome bakery you are greeted with exquisite displays of pastries and cakes and the scent of sugar fills the air, but of course it's the trays of fresh pasta that command my full attention – *ravioli, passatelli, agnolini, quadrucci* – and the most amazing *torta di tagliatelle*, a sweet cake with layers of pastry, nuts and fruit and a topping of egg pasta – *Mamma Mia!*

A few streets away is what Rossana refers to as her pasta lab, the heart of the business, where a group of women shape and fill thousands of pastas every day. It was here that I was shown how to make *agnolini Mantovani*, unique to the region and a shape that reminds me of a little straw hat, the centre stuffed with meat – pork, beef, chicken liver – and which is usually served in broth. Growing up in Poland, I would've eaten something very similar, *tortellini* served in borscht. You can use any dough, but I like to use classic (page 32) or rich egg dough (page 33) for this shape.

Start with a quarter of the dough, keeping the rest in an airtight container, and prepare a tray or baking sheet dusted with coarse semolina, on which to lay out your finished pasta.

Roll out the dough to setting 7 on your pasta machine (page 60).

Lay the dough flat on the work surface or a board and, using a brass *ravioli* cutter, cut out rectangles to a size of 7.5x6cm/3x2.5in.

Pipe a coin-sized amount of filling into the centre of each rectangle (a piping bag gives you a slightly denser filling because it's compressed as it's pushed through the nozzle), but you can use a teaspoon if you prefer.

Now work one by one. Fold the dough in half over the filling, pressing to connect the edges firmly as if you were making *ravioli*. Take the bottom two corners between your finger and thumb, draw them towards you, pinch and seal them together to create your straw hat.

Continue to shape, placing the *agnolini* on the prepared tray until you've used up all of your dough.

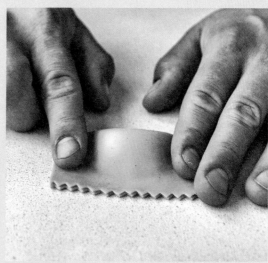
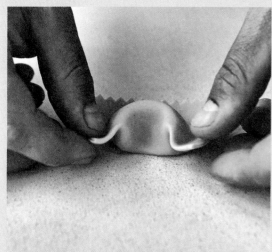
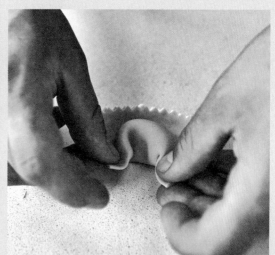

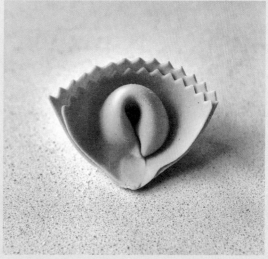

AGNOLINI MANTOVANI WITH PUMPKIN AND AMARETTI

Serves 4

400g/14oz classic egg dough (page 32)

For the filling

600g/1lb 5oz pumpkin, peeled and cut into chunks

30ml/2 tbsp olive oil

30ml/2 tbsp water

40g/1½oz amaretti biscuits, crushed

80g/3oz Parmesan, finely grated, plus extra to serve

grated zest of 1 lemon

For the sauce

90g/3¼oz butter, cubed

handful of sage leaves

When I was talking to my friend Giuseppe about *agnolini Mantovani* – pasta filled with pumpkin, amaretti and *mostarda di frutta* (candied fruits in a mustard syrup) – his eyes took on a dreamy expression at the memory of eating them in Italy. As Giuseppe sells boxes of amaretti in his shop, I bought some to make *agnolini* at home. My recipe doesn't use *mostarda*, as it's hard to come by unless you know of a specialist deli. If you're able to buy it, or you brought some back from a holiday, then you can use it in this filling instead of the lemon zest. Finely chop a teaspoonful, stir it in and taste; you don't want to overpower everything else with the rather strong, spicy flavour.

Preheat the oven to 190°C fan/410°F/gas mark 6. Line a roasting tin with a large piece of kitchen foil, place the chunks of pumpkin into it and drizzle over the olive oil and water. Season with a small amount of sea salt flakes. Now wrap the foil over the top of the pumpkin (this will keep the moisture in as it roasts) and place in the oven. Cook for 20–25 minutes until just soft, then remove from the oven and leave to one side to cool.

When the pumpkin is cool enough to handle, transfer it into a large bowl and combine with the crushed amaretti, Parmesan and lemon zest. Press the mixture with the back of a wooden spoon to break down the chunks of pumpkin and create a paste. Season to taste with sea salt and freshly ground black pepper, then leave the mixture in the fridge to set for a minimum of 30 minutes.

Now roll, fill and shape your pasta (page 222).

Set a large pan of water on the hob and, when the water is boiling, season it generously with table salt. Carefully drop in the pasta and cook for 2–3 minutes.

Meanwhile, melt the butter in a large saucepan with a ladleful of the pasta cooking water. Swirl the pan around to create a butter emulsion, then scoop out the *agnolini* using a slotted spoon and drop into the sauce. Scatter over the sage leaves and swirl again until the sauce thickens a little and the pasta is well coated in the gleaming butter. Share between four warmed bowls and finish with a generous grating of Parmesan.

GNOCCHI

Equipment

dough scraper

garganelli board (optional)

When I was a kid, my grandad Tadek taught me how to play chess. We would sit on the floor together, the chess board between us, a bucket of potatoes on one side, a pan of water on the other, and a plastic bag ready for the potato peelings. Playing chess was a ritual for us, but for him it was also a ritual of peeling potatoes; he always liked to be busy so while I pondered my next move, he could peel a potato, quarter it and drop it in the pan. If I was particularly slow, he'd peel two. See overleaf for the dough ingredients.

The potatoes were used to make soups, mashed to serve in borscht, roasted on a Sunday, or sometimes used to make *kopytka*, often called Polish *gnocchi*, which we would eat with pork or beef *ragù*.

Like *kopytka*, Italian *gnocchi* is a classic comfort food, little pillows of happiness which, depending on the region you are in, will be served with butter and sage, slow-cooked tomato sauce, basil pesto or a meaty *ragù*.

Prepare a tray or baking sheet dusted with flour, ready for your finished *gnocchi* (plain/all-purpose flour will do – just use whatever you have to hand).

To shape the *gnocchi*, take a third of your potato dough (overleaf), place it onto a work surface lightly dusted with flour and then dust again with a little more flour. Using both hands, start to roll from the centre of the dough outwards to create a thick rope about 2.5cm/1in across. Dust the whole length with more flour, then cut into thumb-widths using a dough scraper.

This shape is good to cook as it is, but if you want to create ridged *gnocchi*, place each piece on a *garganelli* board and, using your thumb, gently press down and push away from you across the ridges of the board.

Transfer the finished pasta to the tray and continue until all the dough has been used. If you leave the *gnocchi* on the tray for too long it will become sticky, so it's best to cook them straightaway (see overleaf).

POTATO AND SPINACH GNOCCHI BURRO E SALVIA

Serves 4

For the *gnocchi* dough

1kg/2lb 4oz potatoes, peeled and halved

200g/7oz spinach leaves, washed

1 egg, plus 1 egg yolk

1 tsp table salt

200g/7oz plain (all-purpose) flour, plus extra for dusting

For the butter sage sauce

60g/2¼oz butter, cubed

small handful of sage leaves

40g/1½oz Parmesan, grated, plus extra to serve

lemon juice, to taste

Don't be put off by the number of stages it takes to make *gnocchi*. Wait for a rainy afternoon, listen to your favourite podcast, and make these little pillows of happiness. It's absolutely worth it.

Cut the potatoes into even-sized pieces and place them into a medium pan of cold water. Bring to the boil, then season the water and cook the potatoes for 20 minutes, or until they are cooked through but not too soft (you don't want them to fall apart). Mash the potatoes and allow them to cool.

Meanwhile, blanch the spinach. Bring a pan of water to the boil, drop in the spinach and cook it for no longer than 90 seconds, then immediately transfer it into a bowl of ice-cold water (this will keep the intense green colour of the leaves). When the spinach has cooled, use your hands to squeeze out all the excess moisture, then finely chop and transfer to a large clean bowl.

Weigh out 750g/1lb 10oz mashed potato and add it to the bowl of spinach, then add all the remaining dough ingredients. Use your hands to mix everything together until it starts to form a dough.

Shape the *gnocchi* straightaway (page 226). If you leave the dough to rest it can become quite sticky, so it's best to make and blanch them quickly.

Boil the prepared *gnocchi* in a couple of batches in a large pan of salted boiling water for 1½–2 minutes. You can now leave them on a lightly oiled baking sheet or, if you're ready to eat them, transfer them straight to the sauce.

To make the *burro e salvia*, melt the butter in a large saucepan over a medium heat, then add a ladleful of the *gnocchi* cooking water. Swirl together to create a thin, buttery sauce, and add the *gnocchi* and sage leaves. Reduce the heat slightly, scatter over the grated Parmesan and toss until the cheese has melted into the sauce. Add lemon juice, to taste, and some more pasta cooking water if needed, then season to taste with sea salt and freshly ground black pepper.

I like to serve *gnocchi* in warmed shallow bowls, with a generous chunk of Parmesan so people can help themselves.

MALFATTI

Equipment

muslin cloth (cheesecloth) or linen tea (dish) towel

Ingredients

300g/10½oz ricotta

30ml/2 tbsp olive oil

1 medium onion, finely diced

1 garlic clove, diced

225g/8oz spinach leaves, washed

70g/2½oz Parmesan, finely grated

½ nutmeg, grated

1 egg

50g/2oz fine semolina

These rustic ricotta and spinach dumplings are similar to the more familiar *gnocchi*, but they are much richer, speckled green with the spinach and scented with nutmeg. Also known as *gnudi*, *malfatti* translates as 'badly formed', but don't hold that against them; it's nice not having to worry about making them uniform in size and shape.

Prepare a tray dusted with fine semolina, ready for your finished *malfatti*.

First, strain the ricotta by placing it in a muslin cloth and squeezing it to remove the excess liquid. The ricotta will lose around 10–15 per cent of its overall weight and have a much firmer consistency. Scoop it into a medium bowl and set aside.

Heat the olive oil in a large saucepan and cook the onion and garlic until soft and golden, around 7 minutes on a medium heat. Add the spinach, cover with a lid and cook for 2–3 minutes until the spinach has wilted.

Transfer the spinach mixture to a colander and squeeze any excess liquid out by pressing it hard with a wooden spoon; otherwise, allow it to cool and just squeeze with your hands until the spinach has lost all its moisture.

Finely chop the spinach and add it to the bowl of ricotta along with the Parmesan, nutmeg, egg and semolina. Beat together with a wooden spoon and season to taste. Leave in the fridge to rest and firm for 30 minutes.

When you are ready to shape the *malfatti*, I suggest wetting your hands just a little, as this stops the soft mixture from sticking to them. Shape into walnut-sized balls, placing them on the prepared tray, then slide the tray into the fridge for an hour to firm up (you can leave them overnight if you'd like to prepare them ahead).

MALFATTI WITH SLOW-COOKED TOMATO SAUCE

Serves 4 (makes around 24)

60ml/4 tbsp olive oil

3 garlic cloves, finely chopped

2 x 400g/14oz cans of whole plum or chopped tomatoes

1 batch of *malfatti* (page 230)

To serve

a few basil leaves

Parmesan

These soft dumplings are delicious served in a simple slow-cooked tomato sauce, as I've done here, or tossed in sage butter. I find them quite filling, so you could serve four each to six people as a starter.

In a large saucepan, heat the olive oil, add the garlic and fry for a minute until fragrant, then add the tinned tomatoes. Cook on a medium-low heat for 35–40 minutes, stirring occasionally. Season to taste with sea salt and freshly ground black pepper. Leave on a low heat while you boil the *malfatti*.

Set a large pan of water on the hob and, when the water is boiling, season it generously with table salt. Carefully drop the *malfatti* into the water and cook for 2 minutes, or until they bob to the surface.

Ladle the tomato sauce into four warmed bowls, then, using a slotted spoon, fish out the *malfatti* and place them into the sauce. Alternatively, you can scoop them directly into the pan of sauce and gently mix them together before plating – it's up to you.

Finish with a basil leaf or two and a generous grating of Parmesan.

EXTRUDED & DRIED PASTA

WARM PASTA SALAD
WITH ORZO

Serves 4

300g/10½oz extruded
semolina *orzo* (page 42),
or 250g/9oz dried *orzo*

60ml/4 tbsp olive oil

2 red onions, thinly sliced into
half-moons

4 garlic cloves, finely chopped

300g/10½oz cherry tomatoes,
halved

2 avocados, flesh cubed

grated zest of 1 lemon and
juice of ½ lemon

60g/2¼oz black Kalamata
olives, stoned and halved

bunch of parsley, leaves
picked and finely chopped

bunch of mint, leaves picked
and finely chopped

bunch of basil, leaves picked
and torn

30g/1oz Parmesan, finely
grated

3 tbsp pine nuts, toasted

Vegan option
Replace the Parmesan with
3 tbsp nutritional yeast or
3 tbsp toasted pine nuts

Make this salad when cherry tomatoes are in season and at their
sweetest, then serve it warm for a summer lunch (sunshine optional).
It's best to use ripe Hass avocados, as they have such a creamy
texture and collapse into the warm pasta. You can always pack this
salad to take on a picnic or eat any leftovers for a workday lunch.
If you don't have an extruder to make the *orzo*, just make another
fresh pasta shape or use your favourite brand of dried pasta instead.

Gently warm the olive oil in a large saucepan, add the onion
and garlic and scatter over a large pinch of salt. Stir everything
together, cover with a lid and cook on a medium-low heat for
5 minutes. Take the lid off, stir again, and cook uncovered for a
further 5 minutes. Turn the heat up to medium, add the tomatoes
and cook for 3 minutes, stirring occasionally. When the tomatoes
soften and start to burst a little, take the pan off the heat and set
to one side to cool slightly.

Place the avocado in a large bowl and toss it in the zest and lemon
juice. Add the tomato mixture and the olives and stir everything
together, then set aside while you cook the pasta.

Bring a large pan of water to the boil and season it well with table
salt. Cook the *orzo* for 2–3 minutes until *al dente*. Drain the pasta
and add it to the avocados and tomatoes, along with all the chopped
herbs and the Parmesan. Mix well and season to taste with sea salt
and freshly ground black pepper.

Transfer the salad to a large bowl, preferably set outside for
a summer lunch, and scatter over a handful of toasted pine nuts
just before serving.

BAKED ZITI, VODKA AND SAUSAGE

Serves 4

400g/14oz extruded semolina *ziti* (page 42), or 360g/12½oz dried *rigatoni*

45ml/3 tbsp olive oil

1 onion, diced

2 garlic cloves, finely chopped

1 carrot, diced

2 celery sticks, diced

350g/12oz minced (ground) pork or beef, or sausage meat

90g/3¼oz tomato paste

75ml/5 tbsp vodka

200g/7oz double (heavy) cream

½ tsp chilli flakes

150g/5½oz cooking mozzarella, coarsely grated

Parmesan, to serve

Vegetarian option

Replace the meat with 2 small aubergines (eggplants). Cube the aubergines and fry in olive oil until cooked through and beginning to turn golden. Add to the vegetables with the tomato paste.

Vodka sauce was a popular recipe in my first book, *The Pasta Man*. The creamy chilli sauce makes for top comfort food (although I'm sure the vodka helps too!). With the addition of meat and mozzarella, I hope this baked *ziti* version will be another winner.

Heat the olive oil in a large saucepan and gently sweat the onion, garlic, carrot and celery for 20 minutes until soft and sweet.

In a separate pan, fry the mince or sausage meat on a high heat for 4–5 minutes, turning it over to brown on both sides. You don't want to cook it all the way through, but try to get a nice bit of colour.

Transfer the meat to the pan with the vegetables, add the tomato paste and break up the meat a little with a wooden spoon. Fry for 5 more minutes on a medium heat, so the meat absorbs the flavour of the tomato paste. Don't worry if the paste catches on the bottom of the pan (in the kitchen we always say we're adding more flavour).

Reduce the heat to the lowest setting to avoid lighting the alcohol as you add it. Pour in the vodka, then leave everything to bubble for a few moments before stirring. Add the cream and stir it in, then bring the heat back to medium-low until the sauce starts to bubble again. Scatter over the chilli flakes and season to taste with sea salt and freshly ground black pepper. Leave to one side while you blanch the pasta.

Preheat the oven to 180°C fan/400°F/gas mark 6.

Bring a large pan of water to the boil before adding some table salt, then drop in the *ziti*. Blanch for 20 seconds. (If you're using dried *rigatoni*, cook until *al dente*.) Drain the *ziti*, reserving a jugful of pasta cooking water, and add the pasta to the vodka sauce. Combine everything together in the pan. If the sauce feels a bit too thick, add a splash or two of cooking water to loosen it, then check the seasoning and adjust to your taste.

Now transfer everything to a Pyrex dish or casserole (I use the same dish I bake lasagne in). Scatter the mozzarella over the top and place in the centre of the oven to bake for 15 minutes. Serve with Parmesan to grate at the table and with a fresh green salad on the side.

MAFALDINE WITH SICILIAN PESTO

Serves 4

400g/14oz extruded semolina *mafaldine* (page 42), or 360g/12½oz dried *mafaldine*

45ml/3 tbsp olive oil

2 shallots, finely diced (around 250g/9oz)

2 garlic cloves, finely diced

10 anchovy fillets, from a jar or can

2 tbsp tomato paste

grated zest of 1 lemon

pangrattato (page 248), to serve

I always have onions, garlic and lemons in the kitchen, and a jar of anchovies is another good stand-by, so this just about qualifies as a store-cupboard supper, or at any rate it does in our house. Sometimes all you need to create a beautiful dish is a handful of good ingredients, nothing too fancy. If you're in a hurry, just make the sauce and eat it with your favourite dried pasta.

Heat the olive oil in a large saucepan, add the shallots and garlic and fry on a medium heat for 5 minutes until soft. Add the anchovy fillets and cook for a further 5 minutes, breaking down the anchovies with a wooden spoon. Add the tomato paste and lemon zest and continue to cook on a medium-low heat for 10 minutes, stirring from time to time. Everything will slowly absorb all the flavours and the kitchen will be deliciously fragrant. Leave on a really low heat while you cook the pasta.

Bring a large pan of water to the boil before adding some table salt, then drop in the pasta and cook for 2–3 minutes.

Use tongs to transfer the *mafaldine* into the sauce. Toss everything together a few times, adding more pasta cooking water if the sauce needs loosening a little. Season to taste with sea salt and freshly ground black pepper.

Serve straightaway, topping each plate with herby *pangrattato*.

CONCHIGLIE WITH WILD MUSHROOM AND SAUSAGE RAGÙ

Serves 4

400g/14oz extruded semolina *conchiglie* (page 42), or 360g/12½oz dried *conchiglie*

1 tbsp fennel seeds, toasted

60ml/4 tbsp olive oil

2 onions, diced

1 leek, diced

4 garlic cloves, diced

150g/5½oz wild mushrooms, cleaned and left whole

500g/1lb 2oz sausage meat

400ml/scant 1¾ cups white wine

250ml/generous 1 cup water

70g/2½oz mascarpone

small bunch of parsley, leaves picked and finely chopped

Parmesan, to serve

Use wild mushrooms in this dish, as their earthy autumn (fall) flavour is so distinctive. Look out for chanterelles or girolles, which you should be able to get at a good greengrocer. You can also use a mix of chestnut mushrooms and dried porcini; soak the porcini in the water you're going to use in the *ragù*, which will add every last scrap of their flavour.

It's always worth choosing really good-quality sausages. I like to use pork sausage, preferably one spiced with fennel or coriander seeds. This dish is great to serve with a plate of sautéed spinach alongside; add a touch of chilli and garlic to the greens for an extra kick.

Place the fennel seeds in a dry frying pan (skillet) and cook over a medium heat for about 5 minutes, turning occasionally. When they are toasted and fragrant, set to one side.

In a large saucepan, heat 45ml/3 tablespoons of the olive oil and cook the onion, leek and garlic over a medium-low heat for 20 minutes until soft and slightly golden. Add the wild mushrooms and cook for another 5 minutes until the mushrooms have softened.

Heat the remaining olive oil and fry the sausage meat on a high heat for 4–5 minutes until it starts to go crispy and you get a nice bit of colour. Transfer to the pan with the vegetables, add the toasted fennel seeds, white wine and water, and simmer for 40–45 minutes.

At the end of this time, skim off the excess fat with a slotted spoon, then add the mascarpone and mix well. Season to taste with sea salt and freshly ground black pepper.

Now cook the pasta. Bring a large pan of water to the boil before adding some table salt. Cook the *conchiglie* for 2–3 minutes. Drain the pasta, setting aside a jugful of the pasta cooking water, then add the pasta to the *ragù* and toss everything together. If you think the *ragù* needs loosening a little, simply add half a ladleful at a time of the pasta cooking water. Check the seasoning, scatter the parsley over the saucepan and toss it one more time before serving alongside a chunk of Parmesan so people can help themselves.

EXTRAS & OPTIONS

MEAT BROTH

Serves 4–6

1.5kg/3lb 5oz chicken bones

1.5kg/3lb 5oz beef bones

400g/14oz onions,
roughly chopped

350g/12oz carrots,
roughly chopped

½ head celery, chopped

1 garlic bulb, halved

4 bay leaves

1 tsp black peppercorns

Parmesan rind (optional)

4 litres/8½ US pints
ice-cold water

2 generous sprigs of rosemary

3–4 sprigs of thyme

parsley stalks (optional)

I prefer to make *brodo* with both chicken and beef bones for real depth of flavour, but if you prefer a lighter broth then just use 3kg/6lb 9oz chicken bones. Your butcher will sell soup or stock bones, and roasting them before you add the vegetables and aromatics adds extra flavour too. If you have leek tops or parsley stalks, add them to the pot, and a Parmesan rind if you happen to have one in the freezer (it's always worth saving them).

Preheat the oven to 180°C fan/400°F/gas mark 6.

Place the bones in a large roasting tin (sheet pan) and roast in the oven for 40 minutes until golden brown.

Place the chopped vegetables into a large stock pot with the garlic, bay leaves and peppercorns, adding the Parmesan rind if you have one. Pour in the ice-cold water (this will bring out all the flavours in the pot). Add the roasted bones together with the fat from the bottom of the roasting tin.

Bring the pot to a simmer and leave it to simmer for a minimum of 2 hours, but preferably 4–6 hours: the longer and slower, the better it will be. Skim off the fat from the surface of the stock from time to time.

Add the rosemary and thyme sprigs (and the parsley stalks, if using) to the pot for the last 15 minutes of cooking time. This will add a lovely aromatic flavour to the broth.

Take the pot off the heat and allow it to cool before straining the liquid into a large bowl, discarding the herbs and vegetables. Strain again using a large muslin cloth (cheesecloth) or tea (dish) towel; this will give you a nice clear broth which can now be placed in the fridge to cool completely.

When you are ready to re-heat the broth for cooking, remove and discard the layer of fat which will have settled at the top of the bowl. The broth itself will have the consistency of jelly but will loosen when it's heated up again; this is when to season it with sea salt and freshly ground black pepper.

MEATLESS MEATBALLS

Serves 4

250g/9oz soft white bread, crusts cut off

3 eggs, lightly beaten

1 garlic clove, grated

bunch of parsley, leaves picked and finely chopped

grated zest of 1 lemon

50g/2oz Parmesan, finely grated

vegetable oil, to deep fry

Every food culture seems to have a version of meatballs, whether it's Polish *klopsiki*, Turkish, Greek and Middle Eastern *kofta* or Japanese *tsukune*. This meatless version is based on a Puglian recipe that I got from my friend Luciana; when I tried them at work they proved to be really popular – but then who wouldn't like this hot, oily, flavourful snack?

You can mix up the herbs if you like: try half parsley and half mint for a hint of freshness. And use day-old bread if you can – I like a plain tin loaf – but if the bread is older than that, and very stale, then substitute one egg with 50ml/2 tablespoons of milk and soak the bread in the milk for 5 minutes before making.

Place the soft bread in the bowl of a food processor and pulse until you have rough breadcrumbs (keep the crusts to make breadcrumbs for *pangrattato*, page 248). Transfer the breadcrumbs to a large bowl and add the rest of the ingredients. Mix with a wooden spoon or use your hands to bring everything together – the consistency will be something like stiff mashed potato. Season to taste with sea salt and freshly ground black pepper.

It's best to work with slightly damp hands to avoid the mixture sticking to them. Roll the mixture into walnut-sized balls and place them on a clean tray until you have around 24 lined up.

Use a medium, deep-sided saucepan to fry in batches. Depending on the size of the pan, you will need around 5cm/2in of oil to make sure the balls are covered. Gently heat the oil until a cube of bread sizzles and bubbles when it's dropped in – or use a jam thermometer to check the temperature – it should be between 160/320°F and 170°C/340°F.

Fry the balls, turning them with a slotted spoon until they are golden brown all over. Lift them out onto a plate lined with kitchen paper and fry the next batch.

MALTAGLIATI

Maltagliati – meaning poorly cut – is the name for the rough scraps of dough left over after shaping, and which are well worth saving to use in soups. Frugal cooks would always make sure that nothing was wasted and now, with so many people having a freezer, there's no excuse not to save the scraps (along with any leftover Parmesan rinds) to add to minestrone or a slow-cooked chickpea (garbanzo) soup.

Gather up all the leftovers of dough, cut them to shapes of roughly equal size, and freeze them flat on a tray. Once they are frozen, they can be moved into a suitable container. Alternatively, you can dry them on the work surface by leaving them uncovered for a couple of hours, then place in a freezer bag or box and put them in the freezer.

Maltagliati doesn't need to be defrosted before cooking. Simply drop it into the soup a couple of minutes before you're ready to serve it. The flour from the *maltagliati* will add starch to the soup, thickening it slightly, which I like, but if you prefer, you can thin it out with a little more stock.

PANGRATTATO

It's so useful to keep a box of *pangrattato* in the cupboard, either to add a crunchy finish to a pasta dish or as an ingredient in some pasta fillings. It's a great vegan alternative to Parmesan or pecorino, and I like to scatter it over a dressed green salad, over soup, casseroles or to finish a macaroni cheese.

The Italian for breadcrumbs, *pangrattato* is actually a bit more sophisticated than that, as the seasoning you add gives flavour to the crunch. I like to add garlic, parsley, chilli and olive oil, but you can try your own combinations – thyme and lemon zest, or a tablespoon of rosemary leaves, which goes very well with fish.

Essentially, all you need is to save the ends of a loaf or any stale bread you may have. When you have four or five slices, tear them into pieces and place on a baking sheet. Bake in the oven for

20 minutes at 160°C fan/350°F/gas mark 4. The bread should be nice and browned, but just make sure that it has really dried out.

When the bread has cooled completely, add it to the bowl of a food processor (make sure the bread is not even slightly warm, or it will go soggy when you mix it). Now add 1 small garlic clove, ½ teaspoon of chilli flakes, a drizzle of olive oil and some sea salt flakes. Add a generous handful of picked parsley leaves, then blitz everything together to make coarse crumbs.

Store the *pangrattato* in an airtight container (not in the fridge). It will keep for a week or two, unless you find it addictive, in which case make a bigger batch next time.

GREEN OIL

This herb-infused olive oil is deliciously green and looks stunning drizzled over a pasta dish, on top of a *burrata*, or even on a *panna cotta*.

To make green oil, use herbs like parsley, basil, lovage or coriander (cilantro) (coriander is particularly perfumed); fresh young fig leaves will work too. For pasta dishes I tend to use either a parsley or a basil oil.

Simply blitz equal amounts (by weight) of olive oil and herbs. Use a minimum of 50g/2oz of each and blitz using either a stick or stand blender. Transfer the mixture to a small saucepan and warm slowly to 80°C/175°F (use a jam thermometer or a probe to check the temperature).

The mixture will split slightly in the pan but don't worry, that's what should happen. When the oil has reached the required temperature, take it off the heat and set aside to cool down a little. Set a sieve (strainer) lined with a muslin cloth (cheesecloth) over a bowl, then pour the liquid through it. Leave to drain slowly to create a clear green oil (don't be tempted to press it to try to speed up the job, or the oil will turn cloudy).

Keep the oil in a bottle in the fridge to help retain the bright green colour and use it when you want to finish a special dish.

INDEX

ACKNOWLEDGEMENTS

Producing a book is a team effort combining lots of hard work, skill and fun. The people you share the ride with make all the difference.

Thanks to Elizabeth, for everything.

I am extremely lucky to have such a supportive workplace at 180 Studios. My colleagues love to eat pasta and the kitchen crew are always ready to try new recipes with me.

Dave Brown and Katie Marshall made the long days of the photoshoot whirl by. We had lots of laughs, bagels for breakfast and too much pasta for lunch. The photographs really make me smile. Thanks to Charlie Phillips for sourcing the beautiful props.

To Sarah, Harriet, Claire, Lorraine, Emma, Laura and all of the rest of the team at Quadrille – a huge thank you. It's a pleasure to work with you to produce such amazing books.

Warm thanks to Maya Adiletta at Arcobaleno Pasta for sending the pasta extruder to me. I love to play with it and to make the shapes that aren't possible to make by hand – and the kids think it's the best toy ever!

Sharing a love of pasta has introduced me to so many lovely people around the world and reminds me of all the best things about social media. I'm always so happy to share ideas and inspiration and to see what other people are cooking for dinner. *Buon appetito* to all of you.

AUTHOR BIO

Mateo Zielonka, aka **The Pasta Man** (dubbed so by his Instafans), is head chef at 180 Studios, a collaborative media and arts space in the Strand, London, where he also has his own pasta studio. Polish-born, he has worked in London for 9 years including time at Padella and Polpo. He also teaches pasta classes. You can find some of his pasta videos on Mateo.Kitchen, Food52, The Feedfeed and Designmilk. His previous book *The Pasta Man*, was an instant bestseller.

Scan the QR code below to explore more of Mateo's pasta world.

Managing Director
Sarah Lavelle

Commissioning Editor
Harriet Webster

Art Direction Claire Rochford

Design & Photography
Dave Brown at apeinc.co.uk

Typesetter Seagull Design

Food Stylists
Mateo Zielonka & Katie Marshall

Prop Stylist Charlie Phillips

Head of Production
Stephen Lang

Production Controller
Martina Georgieva

First published in 2023
by Quadrille, an imprint of
Hardie Grant Publishing

Quadrille
52–54 Southwark Street
London SE1 1UN
quadrille.com

Text © Mateo Zielonka 2023
Photography
© Dave Brown 2023
Design and layout
© Quadrille 2023

The rights of Mateo Zielonka
to be identified as the author
of this work have been asserted
by him in accordance with the
Copyright, Design and Patents
Act 1988.

Cataloguing in Publication Data:
a catalogue record for this
book is available from the British
Library.

ISBN: 978 1 78713 963 3

Printed in China

MIX
Paper from
responsible sources
FSC
www.fsc.org FSC™ C020056

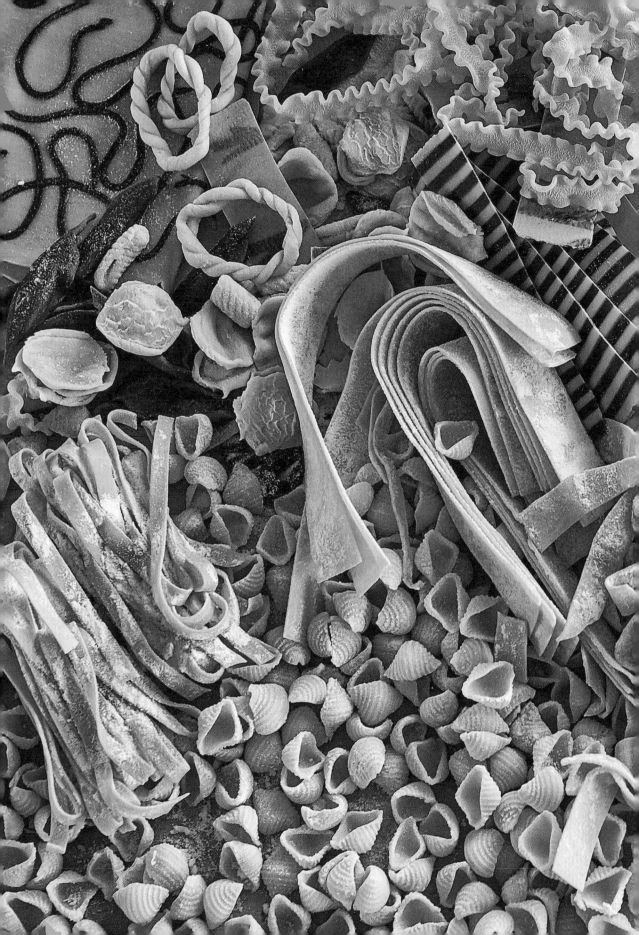